LIFE IN THE
BIBLICAL WORLD

LIFE IN THE BIBLICAL WORLD

Reader's Digest

Published by
THE READER'S DIGEST ASSOCIATION LIMITED
London   New York   Sydney
Montreal   Cape Town

MAN HUNT Assyrian soldiers scramble through reeds hunting an Elamite foe whose army they have just defeated.

LIFE IN THE BIBLICAL WORLD
Edited and designed by Toucan Books Limited
Sole author: Richard Walker

First edition copyright © 1997
The Reader's Digest Association Limited
Berkeley Square House, Berkeley Square,
London W1X 6AB

Copyright © 1996
Reader's Digest Association Far East Limited
Philippines copyright © 1996
Reader's Digest Association Far East Limited
All rights reserved

Printing and binding: Printer Industria Gráfica S.A.,
Barcelona
Separations: Rodney Howe Limited, London
Paper: Perigord-Condat, France

ISBN 0 276 42136 1

**Front cover (clockwise from top left): Boy and
donkey; nomadic encampment; pair of leather
sandals; pomegranate and vine; donkey bearing
baskets; Assyrian monarch Shalmaneser III.**

**Back cover (clockwise from top left): Assyrian
captives; goddess Astarte; shepherd and his flock;
Semitic nomad; figs; jewel box.**

**Page 1: A terracotta Israelite figurine of the 9th or
8th century BC shows a woman kneading dough.**

**Pages 2 and 3: Elamite prisoners enjoy a meal while
their Assyrian guard watches over them.**

CONTENTS

SHOT-PUTTERS   Assyrian soldiers with their slings, in a relief from Nineveh.

STAR POT   Pinched vessels like this one found in Israel were used as oil lamps.

LUTE PLAYER   A female musician from the 7th or 6th century BC.

ANCIENT DICE   Israelite dice testify to a fondness for gaming.

ASSYRIAN SPHINX   The Biblical cherubim may have looked like this carved ivory figure.

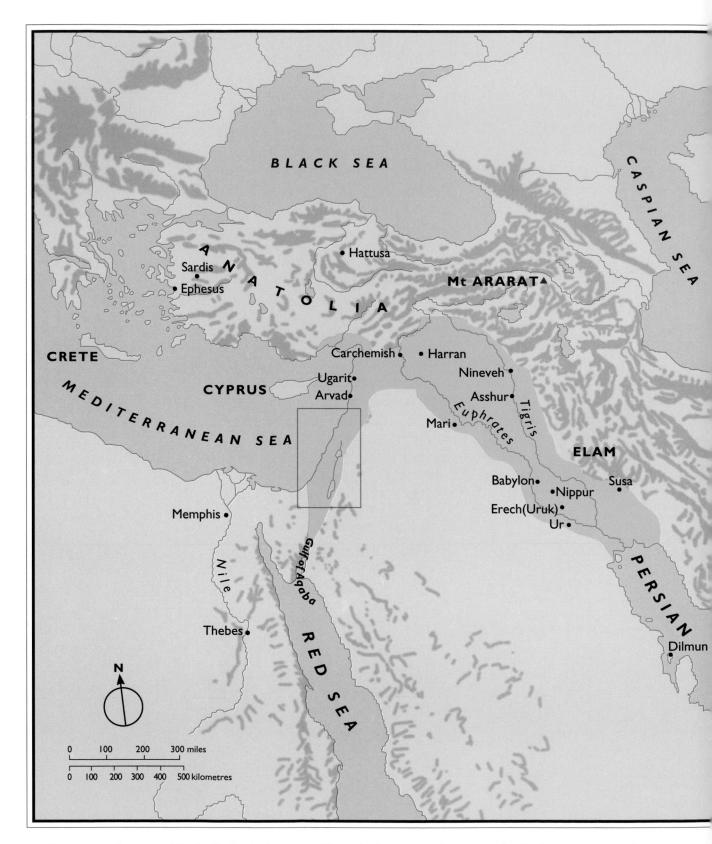

CRESCENT OF FERTILITY   The fertile lands that spread from the Persian Gulf across to the Mediterranean gave rise to some of

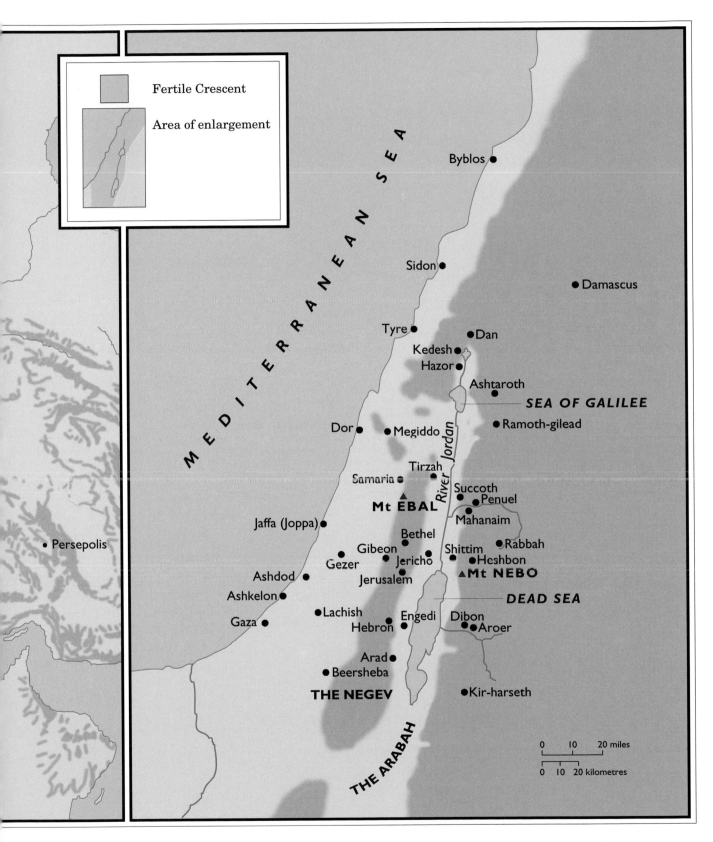

Fertile Crescent

Area of enlargement

Byblos

Sidon

Damascus

Tyre ● Dan

Kedesh

Hazor

Ashtaroth

SEA OF GALILEE

Dor ● Megiddo ● Ramoth-gilead

Tirzah

Samaria ● Succoth

Penuel

Mt EBAL

Mahanaim

Jaffa (Joppa)

Bethel

● Persepolis

Gibeon

Shittim ● Rabbah

Gezer

Jericho

Heshbon

Ashdod

Jerusalem

▲Mt NEBO

Ashkelon

DEAD SEA

Lachish

Engedi

Dibon

Gaza

Hebron

Aroer

Arad

Beersheba

THE NEGEV

Kir-harseth

MEDITERRANEAN SEA

River Jordan

THE ARABAH

0   10   20 miles

0   10   20 kilometres

the world's earliest civilisations. This was the setting in which the Israelites established themselves and became a nation.

FROM ABRAHAM TO MOSES

'Go from your country and your kindred . . . to the land that I will show you,' God commands

Abraham in Genesis. 'And I will make of you a great nation, . . .' From their origins as itinerant herders

and traders, the Israelites did indeed grow to take possession of Canaan, their Promised Land.

WHEN JAMES USHER, a 17th-century Irish archbishop, used Biblical data to calculate the Creation at 9 am on October 23, 4004 BC, nothing was known of the world of the Old Testament other than what the Bible itself had to tell. Since then, scholars and archaeologists have pushed back the darkness, so that even the stalwarts of Genesis are now definable people in a historical setting.

Out of the twilight zone between fact and legend strides Abraham at the head of his family and flocks, the archetypal patriarch. Abraham's kin were semi-nomads practising transhumance, a mobile way of life set by the cycle of the seasons in which herders follow their flocks from summer to winter pastures and back again. They existed in uneasy balance with those who had opted for permanent settlement.

Usually, the balance held, but if it was disturbed – such as by drought – there was disruption as thirsty nomads experimented with settled life.

Ancient tablets record this contrast between herder and farmer, a rivalry as old as Adam and Eve's sons Cain, 'a tiller of the ground', and Abel, 'a keeper of sheep'. The Book of Genesis is firmly on the side of the nomad. It presents city settlements like Sodom and Gomorrah as places of sin and an ambitious building project like the Tower of Babel as an intolerable presumption – an insult to God.

continued on page 12

WANDERER'S LIFE Modern-day Bedouin carry on the traditions of nomadic living practised by Abraham and his kin 4000 years ago.

FOREIGNERS IN PHARAOH'S SERVICE

WE HAVE no definite evidence for the Exodus, but there was no lack of potential candidates. For almost 2000 years, pharaohs and their scribes gloated over the numbers of captives herded into Egypt, and the royal masons were kept busy sculpting such scenes onto the pictorial record. The captives came by land, prodded at the head of returning expeditionary forces, roped, or loaded down with booty. Sometimes we see a kindly soldier helping a faltering woman, or carrying a child on his shoulders. They also came by the boatload and were sometimes sold into slavery by their own rulers.

The records of pharaoh after pharaoh refer to 'stocking the temple workhouse with slaves of His Majesty's captivity'. Statistics survive from the 15th century BC, in particular, when Amenophis II, pursuing a strategy of subjugation by depopulation, carried off 89 600 from Canaan. Others came willingly. The Nile valley, a lush 1000 mile (1600 km) oasis rich in grain, game and fish, acted as a magnet to neighbouring peoples, especially during times of drought or unrest, and whatever the circumstances of their arrival some would not have regretted their fate.

The Egyptians evinced disdain for outsiders: 'sandcrossers' or 'doomed ones' who had to be profoundly grateful for 'the sweet breath of life' which the mere fact of being in Egypt afforded them. But once these 'miserable Asiatics'

PHARAOH OF THE EXODUS
Many scholars think that Ramses II ruled Egypt at the time of Moses.

had Egyptianised their dress and manners, they were quickly absorbed into the mainstream of Nile life and it was possible for those with special skills to prosper.

Pas-Baal, one of 7300 Canaanite captives brought back by Pharaoh Thutmose III, following the Battle of Megiddo in 1482 BC, became chief draughtsman at the great temple of Amun in Thebes and six generations later a descendant of his continued to hold the post. A Hurrian rose to become director of royal construction work and many others with captive origins made their mark in specialist trades.

Hostage sons of vassal rulers from beyond Sinai received training with the pharaoh's personal guard as part of an indoctrination programme and foreign slaves also came to serve the court. Palace records from the 14th century BC cite 'splendid young Canaanite slaves' and 'fine Nyhsyu of Kush shod in white sandals, suitable for bearing sun shades'. By the reign of Akhenaten, around 1350 BC, Canaanites were often serving the pharaoh personally. The job of royal butler became something of a Canaanite speciality.

A few individuals went much further. A certain Ben-ozen from the eastern shores of Galilee was Chief Herald and catering director to Ramses II (often regarded as the pharaoh of the Exodus) about 1250 BC. A high point was reached at the end of that century when a Canaanite with the Egyptianised name of Bay, or Beya, became High Chancellor and power behind the throne in the reign of the polio-afflicted Pharaoh Siptah.

Bay's original name is not known, but his achievements more than match those of Joseph, who in the famous Biblical story becomes chief minister to a pharaoh. Bay, who enjoyed the patronage of a royal widow named Tawosret, bore the title 'Lord of the Entire Land' and even managed to procure for himself a tomb in the Valley of the Kings.

PEOPLES OF THE BIBLE

A bewildering number of peoples jostle through the Old Testament

– some ruling empires, others struggling to keep their freedom.

SOME PEOPLES have left no trace outside a passing Biblical reference. Other names overlap or even duplicate one another.

•AKKADIANS A Semitic people (speaking a Semitic language related to modern Hebrew and Arabic) from Mesopotamia.

•AMORITES (AMURRU) Nomads from Syria who conquered Mesopotamia in the 3rd millennium BC.

•ARAMAEANS Pastoralists from the desert fringes who fanned out over the Fertile Crescent late in the 2nd millennium BC.

•ASSYRIANS Originally a farming

people of Amorite extraction whose homeland was on the upper Tigris.

•BABYLONIANS People from the hot plains of southern Mesopotamia. Their culture was dominant in the Near East through much of the Old Testament period.

•CANAANITES Pre-Israelite occupants of the landbridge between Egypt and Mesopotamia. They were primarily of Amorite descent.

•CHALDAEANS An Aramaean people who drifted farther than most to

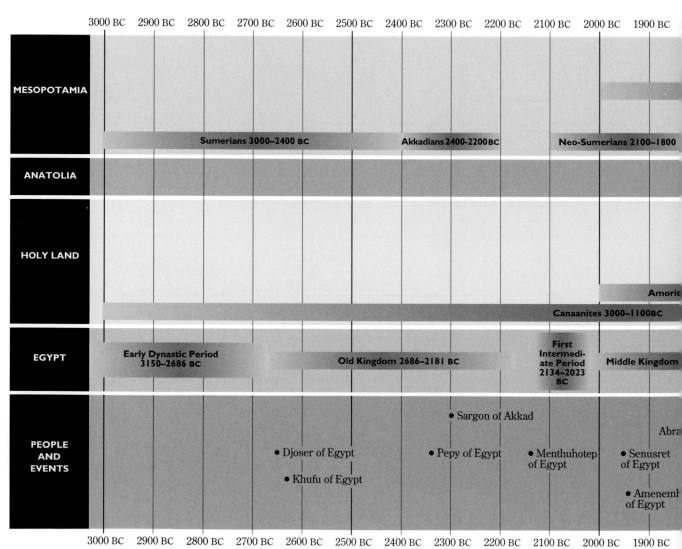

	3000 BC	2900 BC	2800 BC	2700 BC	2600 BC	2500 BC	2400 BC	2300 BC	2200 BC	2100 BC	2000 BC	1900 BC
MESOPOTAMIA	Sumerians 3000–2400 BC							Akkadians 2400-2200 BC		Neo-Sumerians 2100–1800		
ANATOLIA												
HOLY LAND											Amorit	
	Canaanites 3000–1100BC											
EGYPT	Early Dynastic Period 3150–2686 BC			Old Kingdom 2686–2181 BC						First Intermediate Period 2134–2023 BC	Middle Kingdom	
PEOPLE AND EVENTS				• Djoser of Egypt • Khufu of Egypt				• Sargon of Akkad • Pepy of Egypt		• Menthuhotep of Egypt	• Senusret of Egypt • Amenemh of Egypt	Abra

| | 3000 BC | 2900 BC | 2800 BC | 2700 BC | 2600 BC | 2500 BC | 2400 BC | 2300 BC | 2200 BC | 2100 BC | 2000 BC | 1900 BC |

RISE AND FALL The great Mesopotamian empires rose, fell and sometimes rose again. Lesser realms, such as Israel, enjoyed

settle in the south of Mesopotamia. Babylon was ruled by a Chaldean dynasty in the 6th century BC.

•HITTITES Warriors from beyond the Caucasus whose empire reached the edge of Canaan from a stronghold in the heart of modern Turkey.

•HURRIANS People from the mountains above Mesopotamia.

•LYDIANS Their nation on the west coast of Turkey emerged after the breakup of the Hittite Empire.

•MEDES Horse-herding twins to the

Persians with whom they created a larger empire than any before it.

•MOABITES Their kingdom, perched on a fertile plateau east of the Dead Sea, constantly fluctuated in size according to the fortunes of war.

•PERSIANS Emigrants from the northern Russian steppes who settled in the west of modern Iran and eclipsed the Assyrians and Babylonians to forge an empire stretching from Egypt to India.

•PHILISTINES Allied to Aegean sea

rovers, they were beaten back from an attempted incursion into Egypt and settled along the Mediterranean coast.

•PHOENICIANS Seafaring descendants of the Canaanites occupying what is now Lebanon. They were consummate middlemen who dotted the Mediterranean and beyond with trading colonies.

•SUMERIANS Mysterious, brilliantly inventive pioneers of urban living in southern Mesopotamia.

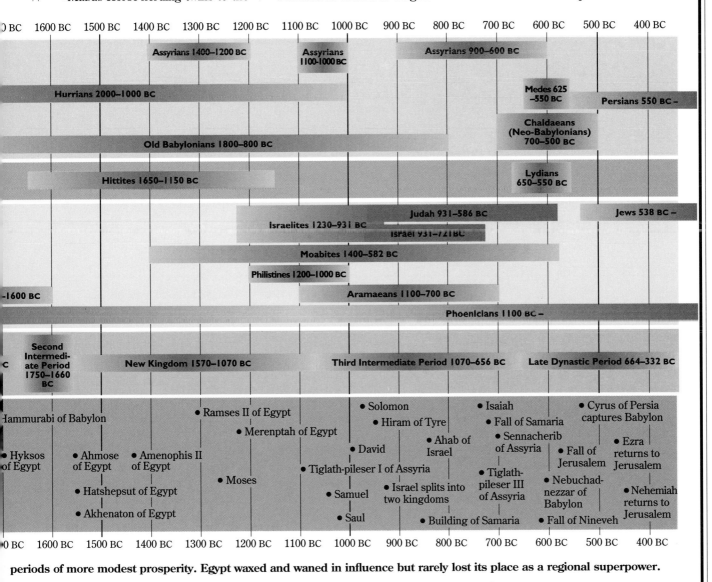

periods of more modest prosperity. Egypt waxed and waned in influence but rarely lost its place as a regional superpower.

SHEEP AND GOATS These herders are Sumerians from around 2750 BC, depicted on a panel found at Ur.

When Cain the settled farmer makes a sacrificial offering of fruit, it is rejected out of hand, while Abel's sacrifice of spring lamb is accepted. Jealous and resentful, Cain kills Abel, and gets cursed to eternity.

THE WORLD OF GENESIS

Genesis takes us on a grand tour of the ancient world, from the Garden of Eden, past the Tower of Babel, down to Egypt. Eden was 'eastward', the Bible says, at the source of great rivers. Candidate sites include somewhere in the bird-dappled marshlands at the head of the Persian Gulf. Some scholars see in Adam and Eve's expulsion from this idyllic spot a reflection of the beginnings of agriculture, when a brave few abandoned hunting and foraging for the risks and toil of planting and tilling.

By the evidence of his itinerary and lifestyle, Abraham could be dated anywhere between 2500 and 500 BC, but scholars generally place him around 1750. They call the region he traversed the Fertile Crescent, though it is better imagined as a triangle, contained by mountain and desert on two sides and sea on the third and extending from the tip of the Persian Gulf to the Mediterranean; it encompasses modern Iraq, Syria, Lebanon, Jordan, Israel and the Nile delta. It was the cradle of Western civilisation.

Dividing the triangle, two rivers, the Euphrates and Tigris, slant through what is now an arid brown plain, bearing the life force of water impregnated with rich silt – sometimes not enough and sometimes in dangerous abundance, for in springtime they are charged with the snow-melt of the mountains. This precarious plenty of Mesopotamia – the 'land between the rivers' as the Greeks dubbed it – provided the right combination of challenge and opportunity to lure early herders and farmers from the foothills into extraordinary creative endeavour. Here were invented or developed irrigation, the wheel, mathematics, astronomy and writing.

Riverside villages burgeoned into the first cities, each with its protective god. But the gods provided no protection against human rivalry. Cities fighting over water resources became prey to invaders who absorbed their achievements and carried them further. In this way, Mesopotamia's earliest known inhabitants, the Sumerians, were overrun around 2300 BC by the Akkadians, a Semitic people – that is, speaking a Semitic language related to modern Arabic and Hebrew – from the northern edge of Mesopotamia. The Sumerians had lived in cities, but it was the Akkadian king Sargon I who united the river plain under one rule. His empire lasted about

LAND OF MILK AND HONEY The fertile valleys of Canaan attracted successive waves of invaders, before and after the arrival of the Israelites.

SUBJECT PEOPLES Israelite porters deliver tribute to the Assyrians at one of the low points in their nation's history.

250 years, to be replaced by a new Sumerian realm centred at Ur, one of Mesopotamia's oldest cities.

By about 1900 BC, the dominant people in Mesopotamia were Amorites, another Semitic folk. They had taken possession from the desert fringes, and under their influence a new city grew in importance: Babylon. Other peoples were also moving onto the scene – Hurrians from the mountainous north-east and Hittites from beyond the Caucasus.

FROM UR TO THE PROMISED LAND

The Amorites were well advanced into the process of settlement and assimilation when the family of Abraham – Semites like the Amorites – moved base from Ur up the Euphrates to Harran. They may have been seizing the opportunity of improved trading conditions since Harran was a major caravan junction in Hurrian territory at the top of the plain.

From Harran, the Bible has Abraham, his relatives and descendants strike out on careers as shepherds, itinerant craftsmen, tinkers and traders. They made a base for themselves in hilly country above the Mediterranean and ventured in little family groups as far as Egypt, where they prospered for some time, only to be enslaved when

the political climate changed. Their escape in a great migration known as the Exodus was crowned by the conquest of their Promised Land – the hilly country first spied out by Abraham.

The period between Abraham's wanderings and the Exodus is generally put at around 500 years, though some scholars make it less. The historical record is of no help: in all of the writings of Ancient Egypt and Mesopotamia that have come to light, no mention of either event has yet been found.

But we do have a clear picture of the turbulent period in which the Israelite nation emerged, and of its conditions of life. The Promised Land is a tiny, geographically tormented territory, hardly the size of Wales. It lies wedged between sea and desert, with hills high enough for winter snow. Its inside edge is dug into the deepest land trench on earth where the Jordan river feeds a salt lake, the Dead Sea, whose surface is 1299 ft (396 m) below sea level. This was part of a larger region known as Canaan, which provided a land bridge between Mesopotamia and the Nile. It was isolated from the Nile by 110 miles (180 km) of rock and sand – the Sinai desert.

Long before Abraham's time, the Canaanites had prospered. Hundreds of farming hamlets dotted the

DAYS, MONTHS, YEARS: MEASURING TIME AND MOTION

TIME did not exist as an abstract concept but was seen in terms of its content – the seasonal agricultural cycle, phases of the moon and events great and small.

Ways of keeping track of the years varied. The Egyptians numbered theirs according to the reign of the current pharaoh, starting afresh with each accession. The Israelites likewise dated each reign apart. The Assyrians named their years after important persons and the Babylonians after big events, such as campaigns.

Calendars were lunar-based, regulated by priestly observation of the moon. The sighting of the new crescent moon marked the passage from one month to the next. The 11 day lag between 12 lunar months and the natural – solar – year was a constant problem that only the early Egyptians were able to bridge. They did so by observation of the star Sirius whose appearance chanced to coincide with the annual rising of the Nile. They found that this happened on average once every 365 days. Accordingly, by 2600 BC, they had adjusted their lunar calendar to 12 months of 30 days plus five feast days to welcome the rising waters of their New Year. Without leap years to accommodate the extra fraction of a day, the Egyptian calendar drifted through a complete cycle of seasons every 1460 years.

The Mesopotamians clung to the dictates of the moon. Whenever the months and seasons began to slip apart, it was a royal responsibility to order an adjustment. Kings like Hammurabi would declare a 'gap' year and repeat a month to restore a rough synchronisation. Eventually Babylonian astronomers were able to calculate the exact lengths of lunar months and come up with a solution. They computed a periodic cycle of 235 lunar months that fell into step with the natural cycle over 19 years. Some time after 500 BC this was adopted in the form of 12 years of 12 months interspersed with seven 13 month years.

To calibrate day and night, the Mesopotamians adopted the same 12-1 ratio as for the months of the year. The Babylonian 'hour' was consequently a double-hour, subdivided into 60 double-minutes. This could be tracked in sunlight by a shadow-clock, ancestor of the sundial, or at any time by a water clock.

The Israelites were haphazard in their reckonings and had no words for hour or minute, although they eventually adopted the Babylonian system. Their early calendar followed the agricultural cycle, but after their return from Babylonian exile in the 6th century BC, cultural crosscurrents led them to number their months from the new moon of spring, yet celebrate New Year upon the autumn equinox, the turning point of their farming year.

Distances were expressed in terms such as a day's travel or the range of a bow-shot.

The Babylonian 'mile' was the distance that could be covered on foot in a double-hour, the same word being used for both – *beru*. It was about 6 miles (10 km). Other measurements used anatomical references – the width of a palm, the span from outstretched thumb to little finger and the cubit, derived from the distance from elbow to fingertip: about 20 in (50 cm).

HEAVENLY SIGNS The stars and crescent moon on this Babylonian 'boundary stone' are symbols of the gods. The Mesopotamians were careful observers of the heavens who gave many constellations the names they still bear.

ON THE OX-CART Prisoners and booty are carried off after a successful Assyrian siege of the Israelite city Lachish.

valleys, each within an easy day's walk of a protective walled town. This prosperity was cut short by the same forces that kept Mesopotamia in upheaval: uncertain harvests and incursions from the north. The Canaanites also had to contend with the Egyptians, whose rulers dispatched expeditionary forces into Canaan to 'pacify' its inhabitants. Pharaoh Thuthmose III in a brilliant campaign around 1500 BC pacified Canaan. Many towns were emptied and their people dragged off to servitude in Egypt. Princes were required to take an oath of loyalty and dispatch their sons to Egypt as hostages.

Outlaw bands known as Hapiru operated from the hills. This term, possibly meaning 'dust-raisers' (in the sense of people prone to making hasty exits), had been employed for centuries to describe semi-independent communities of freebooters. In the Canaan of the 14th century BC, they seemed to be everywhere, raiding towns, playing off prince against prince while enticing their slaves to revolt. They were strongest around Shechem, a fortress town guarding a strategic defile north of Jerusalem. Abraham 'passed through' this way and according to the Bible this is where the Israelites under Joshua would gather formally to found their nation. Some scholars see in Hapiru the origin of the name Hebrew.

A cache of 14th-century BC diplomatic dispatches has survived and we can follow in graphic detail the violent squabbles of the governor-princes of states that would loom large in the Bible story – Ashkelon, Damascus, Gaza, Gezer, Megiddo, Shechem, Jerusalem. In their dispatches they dutifully profess loyalty to Egypt, while accusing one another of treacherous dealings with the Hapiru.

The Prince of Jerusalem, a loyal pharaoh's man, is in all kinds of trouble. His small garrison of Sudanese troops is getting out of hand – 'I was almost killed in my own house!' he protests – and he begs for reinforcements to be sent posthaste from one of Egypt's coastal bases. 'Send archers . . .

send archers', he pleads, but the situation only worsens. Bethlehem, 5 miles (8 km) away, goes over to the enemy. The dispatches cease, the outcome unrecorded.

During the next century, the Egyptians tried to enforce tighter control with a stronger military presence and regular sweeps. A grey granite memorial commemorates such a search-and-destroy mission undertaken in about 1220 BC by Pharaoh Merenptah. After extolling the reduction of three Canaanite towns comes the startling boast: 'Israel lies desolate; its seed is no more'. This is the first evidence outside the Biblical text of the existence of an entity known as Israel. The only further clue is in the style of hieroglyphic, which indicates that this 'Israel' is a group or a tribe as distinct from a settled community.

THE ISRAELITES MAKE THEIR STAND

Shortly thereafter the Near East was convulsed, in part by an invasion from across the Mediterranean of Aegean and other northern folk. These sea rovers had been harrying the Nile delta for some time, but shortly after 1200 BC they came in force, intent upon settlement, not just plunder.

Around the eastern seaboard they advanced, until halted in sea and land battles at the approaches to Egypt – in which, confusingly, some of them fought for the Egyptians as mercenaries. The attackers reeled back, scattering across the Mediterranean, but some settled on the coastal plain where they consolidated around their most numerous clan, the Peleset, later known as the Philistines.

Other destabilising factors were also at work around this time, though exactly what they were is still a puzzle for scholars. One possibility is that a natural disaster, a series of catastrophic earthquakes, say, struck the region, leaving many cities in ruins. Whatever the case, when the chaos subsided, the balance of power in the eastern Mediterranean had collapsed. Egypt alone remained intact, but it was severely weakened.

Aramaeans, a previously insignificant but suddenly vigorous tribal group, seized the chance to carve out states of their own in northern Canaan. The Philistines burst forth from their coastal strongholds. The Canaanites were left in control of upper Galilee, the plain of Jezreel and other lowland areas. In a narrow maritime strip tucked behind high cedar-decked mountains, the Phoenicians established themselves as merchant voyagers based in cities such as Sidon, Tyre and Byblos.

What of the hills that had sustained the Patriarchs' sheep? Here much-buffeted folk with bitter memories of the Egyptians were forging a tribal alliance: we encounter and confirm at last the Israelites. Hemmed in by the superior arms of the Philistines, they would rely upon guerrilla warfare and a covenant struck with their protective deity Yahweh, or Jehovah. It would be a hard bargain, the impact of which reverberates through book after book of the Old Testament, and it reverberates still.

AFTER MOSES

According to the Biblical account, a series of 'judges', emerging through force of personality, usually in times of emergency, led these early Israelites. They included figures like Gideon, who brought victory over the Midianites. They also included a woman, Deborah, who saw off Jabin, Canaanite King of Hazor to the north, and his commander-in-chief Sisera.

Later, this arrangement gave way to rule by kings, the first two, Saul and David, chosen by the last of the judges, Samuel. Saul, wilful and erratic, died in battle against the Philistines. David, his archrival whom he had jealously banished from his court, became the next king. He went on to capture Jerusalem and made it capital of a new and unified realm. This lasted barely 100 years. David was a southerner,

POTTERS' STYLE Canaanite pots testify to a flourishing culture.

PLUMED HELMETS Philistine warriors (above) on a 12th-century BC Egyptian relief wear their distinctive battle headgear. A bronze statuette (right) of about the same era portrays a Canaanite god, possibly Baal.

from Bethlehem, who never fully won the loyalty of Israel's northern tribes. After the death around 931 BC of his son Solomon – under whom the united kingdom reached the height of its glory – the northern tribes broke away to form their own separate state. This called itself Israel, ruled by a succession of dynasties from its capital Samaria. David's descendants reigned in Jerusalem over the rump kingdom of Judah.

Both states had periods of expansion and prosperity but, in a region dominated by the rise and fall of great empires, neither could expect to be left in peace. After many ups and downs, Samaria fell to the Assyrians in 721 BC, Jerusalem to the Babylonians in 587 BC, and in both cases their upper classes were deported. In 538 BC some of the exiles started returning to Jerusalem. Many others stayed scattered across the Near East where they formed communities in most of its great cities.

The Near East by then was very different from the region wandered by Abraham and his kin more than 1000 years before. Empires had come and gone and all had now tumbled before the might of the Persians ruling a vast realm from India to North Africa and Asia Minor. Where Abraham had roamed with his flocks, his Israelite descendants in their Promised Land had slowly learned the arts of settled agriculture. Now their descendants had spent half-a-century as exiles in one of the Near East's most glittering cities, Babylon, acquiring much of its sophistication.

Yet certain factors remained the same, ruling the lives of ordinary people from generation to generation. As in the desert long ago, the family, clan and tribe were all-important, ensuring help when help was needed. Most importantly perhaps, the austere values of the desert survived in the Scriptures and religion that composed the Jewish people's most enduring legacy to humankind.

LIFE IN TOWN AND COUNTRY

Daily life for most Israelites was the life of villages and hamlets. By 1000 BC they had largely abandoned the wandering existence of their nomadic forebears and were diligently tilling and terracing the hills of their Promised Land or herding flocks of sheep and goats. Unlike the great metropolises of Egypt or Mesopotamia, the Israelites' cities were small, cramped, fortified places, and even among city-dwellers, the majority went out into the fields each day to tend their crops or flocks.

LIFE ON THE LAND

Water dictated the patterns of the farming year. Rain falling in the winter months and

springs bubbling up from the limestone hills enabled the Israelites to reap

the bounty of barley, wheat, olives, vines and figs.

THE OLD TESTAMENT offers us a clear vision of the good life: 'Every man under his vine and under his fig tree.' The Bible is tireless in describing the Promised Land 'of wheat and barley, and fig trees and pomegranates, a land of olive oil and honey', and the Biblical writers were not the first to use such glowing terms. An Egyptian traveller left a fuller and remarkably similar description early in the 2nd millennium BC. It was 'a good land', he wrote. 'Figs were in it, and grapes. It had more wine than water. Plentiful was its honey, abundant its olives. There were all kinds of fruit trees. Barley was there, and wheat. There was every kind of cattle.'

This was not, however, the lush plenty of the Nile valley, nor the carefully managed surpluses of the Mesopotamian river rims. His comment 'more wine than water' implied a snag; fertility offset by the ever-present threat of drought.

The Israelites occupied a narrow upland strip about 150 miles (240 km) long. The hills were all

carefully terraced and gashed through with deep, fertile valleys whose greenery and shade eased the sun's glare. The ubiquitous olive, and fruit trees, endured where other crops could not. The hills let down gently to the Mediterranean in the west, where the warm, humid plain was dotted with Philistine strongholds. Farther north, Phoenician ports were tucked under the Lebanon range.

To the east, beyond the Jordan chasm, a tableland caught rain at its edge but soon the terrain became lost in the Arabian desert. Along the fertile rim of the plateau lay the grain and grazing lands of Moab, Ammon and Aram, which were able in places to sustain woods of oak and pine, and the river-irrigated gardens of Damascus.

Away to the north, a ten day caravan trek beyond Damascus, wound the upper Euphrates, and beyond that the Tigris river watered the homeland of the Assyrians – 'a land like your own land', an Assyrian negotiator advised besieged citizens of Jerusalem, as he tried to coax them into surrender: 'A land of corn and wine, bread and vineyards, olive oil and honey.'

Downriver from Assyria lay fabulous Babylon and the sun-baked flood plain that nurtured Ur and the other early city-states, reaching to the Persian Gulf.

PROMISE AND REALITY

Some scholars believe that the name Jordan means 'Descender'. That meaning would certainly be appropriate. From snow-fed mountain slopes, the river plummets to the midget 'Sea' of Galilee, thence to the salty sump of the Dead Sea. Where brine gives way to a thorn and tamarisk entanglement, the

STONY GROUND The bare hills of the Judaean desert are a reminder of the wildernesses roamed by the Israelites' ancestors. Even when settled in their fertile land, deserts like these were never far away.

FARMING IN STEPS   Careful terracing meant that even the steepest Judaean hillsides could be cultivated.

badlands of the Arabah arise and reach down to the Gulf of Aqaba, forefinger of the Red Sea. On their eastern flank, the Biblical land of Edom faded into the desert and a string of oases pointed the way to distant Saba (Sheba). In the other direction, beyond Beersheba, the Promised Land petered into the barren Negev and beyond that the arid rocks and gulches of Sinai were a last barrier between promise and the fulfilling bounty of the Nile delta.

The land's 'promise' was imparted by rains that fell steadily in the winter months. For six summer months, it was (and is) hot and bone dry – scorching on days when the sirocco, the sand-laden desert wind, blows in from Arabia. But the hills are limestone and form a natural reservoir from which numerous springs gush forth like the ones which gave life to the cities of Jericho and Jerusalem. For the rest, strict conservation was the rule of life.

AHIYU: A LANDLORD IN JERUSALEM

AHIYU and three of his sons were snoring in the farmhouse's upper chamber – and their motley retinue were camped in the courtyard. The party had come from Jerusalem to Gezer the day before and were staying with Ahiyu's brother-in-law Benaiah. Ahiyu had prospered, thanks to connections born of a tenuous claim to descent from the royal house of David, and some lack of scruple. By encouraging the ambitions of his relatives until they over-reached themselves, he now controlled three farms and a vegetable garden outside the walls of Jerusalem, which the previous owner (a cousin of his wife) worked as his tenant. Benaiah owned his land but relied on Ahiyu to sell his crops.

King Josiah of Judah was trying to enforce economic reforms aimed at limiting the kind of land-grabbing that was causing such distress. But kings had tried this before. To get around the new regulations against charging interest on debts, Ahiyu simply used heavier weights on his scales when exacting repayments.

The guests eventually woke and came down the steps, drawn by the smell of new-baked bread. Benaiah's wife had her daughter Miriam oiled and scented and engaged in housework, in hopes of encouraging Ahiyu's interest in making a match for his unmarried son. Though it was now considered sinful, she discreetly clasped for good luck a little figurine of the 'Queen of Heaven', the goddess Asherah.

Ahiyu's servants loaded Benaiah's olive crop onto an ox-cart and after paying cursory respects at the family shrine, Ahiyu set forth, mounted on a donkey. The party was joined by others to make up an impromptu caravan for the easy, three-hour amble down the dusty slopes to Ekron, a Philistine city that had boomed under the Assyrian yoke.

Olives were delivered to one of Ekron's many oil mills – the astute Assyrians had concentred regional production here. Ahiyu watched the millstones grinding and pulp being squeezed under great weights.

That evening, while his sons went off to inspect the temple of Baal-zebub, Ahiyu had an appointment with a Phoenician merchant who had an interesting proposition about the export of perfume from the oasis of Engedi on the Dead Sea. They talked and drank strong wine late into the night, discussing news such as the designs the Assyrians had on Egypt. Ahiyu was aware that any rash move by his king and tiny Judah could be snuffed out, taking his ambitions with it.

Bleary-eyed, Ahiyu turned in for the night. He would set out for home in the morning, taking a fine Phoenician robe for his demanding wife and a trinket for a favourite serving girl.

FRUIT OF THE LAND **A merchant departs having bought a farmer's olive crop, now stowed in baskets on two oxen.**

FIG

POMEGRANATE

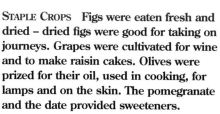

DATE

VINE

OLIVE

STAPLE CROPS Figs were eaten fresh and dried – dried figs were good for taking on journeys. Grapes were cultivated for wine and to make raisin cakes. Olives were prized for their oil, used in cooking, for lamps and on the skin. The pomegranate and the date provided sweeteners.

Underground cisterns were hacked out of the rock to catch and store the winter rains. Dregs remaining by the end of summer must have been foul bilge, but every drop was precious.

Throughout the ancient Near East, clean spring water was something to conjure with. The Biblical David evinces such longing for a drink from the best well in his hometown, Bethlehem, that three of his men slip through enemy lines to fetch him some. Later Persian emperors refused to stomach local water supplies while on campaign and travelled with tanker carts of 'golden water' (boiled as a precaution) from Susa. Once back at home, they perversely

demanded water from the farthest limits of their domains – from the Nile and even the Danube.

Marshalling, maximising and protecting limited resources were the driving forces of communal existence. Among the Israelites, romantic nostalgia for the roving lifestyle persisted among groups of zealots calling themselves Rechabites, who made a cult of living in tents and would have nothing to do with agriculture, but they were an extremist fringe.

FARMING THE HILLS

The Israelites' survival depended upon the hard graft of peasant farming and on all that could be got from barley and wheat, sheep and goat, ox and donkey, olive, vine and fig. All endeavour was centred upon village units, which began to even appear in some of the more daunting terrain as irrigation techniques slowly improved.

Hills were progressively stripped of much of their tree cover and terraced, even in the arid Negev, to conserve the thin soil and improve water distribution. The spread of iron tools from around the 11th century BC quickened the process of clearing land

COME TO THE WATERS Grooves in the stone at the mouth of this Judaean well testify to the ropes used by generations of villagers to draw water from it.

BAKE OR BREW?

Near Eastern folk learned the arts of fermentation even before they had domesticated grain and the grape, scholars suspect. There is lively debate over which came first – bread or beer.

PASTORAL CARE   The shepherd led his sheep to watering and grazing sites and protected them from wild beasts.

and cutting channels and reservoirs. A method of sealing cisterns with a lime cement stopped seepage.

Nothing was wasted. Straw from winnowed grain was gathered up for winter fodder and what chaff remained was rotted with dung to manure the fields, or else the mixture was dried for fuel. The olive was a provider of food, light, cooking oil, medicine and skin cleanser. In Mesopotamia where the olive did not grow, sesame was substituted.

One word for cattle originally meant 'possessions' and referred equally to all kinds of domestic beast – sheep, goat, ox or ass. The sheep was by far the most important, for its fleece more than its flesh, of which the distinctive fat tail was the

FAITHFUL OX
A relief from Nineveh shows an ox and a woman carrying a water skin.

choicest part. The donkey (ass) was the vital beast of burden. The ox hauled both cart and plough, and was slaughtered for meat on special occasions only. Horses – imported from Egypt and Anatolia – were too costly in upkeep for anything but war.

The availability of water dictated the patterns of life. In Mesopotamia, the annual river flood around June set in motion a sophisticated process of irrigated agriculture. For the Israelites, the agricultural year began late in October, when the early or 'former' rains began to break up the baked ground for ploughing and sowing. Then the 'latter' rains brought on the crops in March.

PLEASURES OF SPRINGTIME
Springtime quickened the pulse, especially of those who had been cooped up in the dank, malodorous cities. Anemones and cyclamen painted the hillsides and

flowering shrubs softened the harshness of the highlands with scents of thyme and sage. First the almond blossomed; after that, the pomegranate exploded into vivid scarlet, and the fig sprouted green nobs on its bare boughs. Then the Israelite was moved to poetry and, in the Song of Solomon, rhapsodised on romance and beauty:

Rise up, my love, my fair one, and come away.
For, lo, the winter is past, the rain is over and gone;
The flowers appear on the earth; the time of singing is come,
And the voice of the turtle dove is heard in our land;
The fig tree ripeneth her green figs,
And the vines are in blossom,
They give forth their fragrance.

But spring was cruelly short, and soon the sirocco would burn off the fresh pasture and sometimes also the shoots of new crops, if a late downpour had not already washed them away.

Flax was a winter crop harvested early; then came barley from late April and wheat a few weeks after the barley. The precious vines were pruned in spring and lovingly tended and guarded for picking from July to October. The main fig crop came in August or September, and finally the gnarled olive trees gave

TUCKING IN Feasters use their hands to scoop up food from a common dish in this Assyrian relief.

up their harvest, which ran into the next planting season. Poor rains, a locust swarm, or an invading army could at any time break the cycle and turn sufficiency into famine.

THE PROBLEM WITH PORK

THE PIG is an excellent source of meat, so why did the Israelites and other peoples of the ancient Near East make pork taboo?

Early Sumerians set restrictions on pig-eating, and so did the Egyptians. In Babylonia, pork was taboo to the gods, but people ate it all the same. In the cities pigs scavenged domestic garbage and must have provided the poor with their main opportunity for a square meal.

According to the Bible, Moses received a divine instruction to treat the pig as 'unclean'. Long before this in Egypt, the pig was one of several animals associated with particular gods and taboo to the rest. According to one Egyptian myth, the god Seth disguised himself as a pig and gored his rival Horus in the eye. The creator god Re thereupon declared the pig to be 'an abomination'.

Bans on pig meat were believed to stem originally from concerns that it could harbour dangerous parasites in warm climates, but nowadays anthropologists seek a social cause. They point out that the pig is useful only for its flesh.

It could neither be milked nor ridden, could not pull a plough or carry a load, and it could not be herded like cattle, sheep or goats. The pig's natural habitat was the edge of swamps, forests and along river banks. Once removed from there it had to be fed grain or foodstuffs that people might otherwise eat. Pastoral nomads would feel a jealous resentment towards settled people with the means to raise such an abundant meat source which by its nature was denied to them.

The consequence, anthropologists reason, was a taboo which registered most strongly within societies that kept alive traditions associated with their nomadic roots: in particular, the Israelites.

The dangers of the wilderness, too, were everywhere only a step away. The lion gets 130 mentions in the Bible; it was a subspecies, now extinct, less formidable than today's African lion, but a menace nonetheless. The bear was much feared; leopard, wolf, jackal and hyena were constant threats to livestock, and snake or scorpion an ever-lurking hazard. Livestock might be penned within the village at night.

FRUGAL FOOD

Fare was austere, and a juicy steak or lamb roast was a treat for special occasions, usually associated with a religious sacrifice. The orange and other citrus fruits, stalwarts of the modern Israeli economy, had yet to reach the Near East and the tomato, potato and maize would not be known until their discovery in America thousands of years hence.

The domestic hen did not reach the region from South-east Asia until late in the period. The 'fatted fowl' of Solomon's table was a wild goose, or it might even have been a cuckoo. The Biblical 'apple' was a

STONE CRUSHED This olive press, from the 3rd century BC, was dug up in the hills south-west of Jerusalem.

quince or an apricot. Sugar was another unknown, but through Old Testament times the honey bee, originating in southern Europe, spread southwards, providing one form of sweetener. The bountiful date palm, restricted to hot river valleys, provided another – the mushy essence of dates, which was made by pounding the fruit into a pulp.

A scarcity of water called for alternative ways to slake thirst. Milk – from goats or sheep – did not stay fresh for long, but people knocked back the sour curd. Pomegranate juice was one of the favourite summer thirst quenchers and the juice of the first ripe figs was a special delicacy.

Everybody drank wine and beer or ale – everybody but the Rechabites. It was normally diluted but sometimes spiked with spices and ingredients that increased its potency. Fermentation happened quickly under the hot September sun and the wine was ready for drinking after 40 days. The sediment ('lees') had by then settled and the wine was poured off into big earthenware jars, sealed with pitch, or into stoppered goatskin bags, the Israelite's bottle. Date wine was popular with the Babylonians.

DINNER AT SUNSET

Cooking implied stewing rather than roasting. Esau's 'mess of pottage', a thick lentil soup, was typical fare. Vegetable patches next to the homestead provided essential vitamin supplements from cucumbers, leeks,

---

TOAST OF THE TOWN

A 3500-year-old loaf of bread was found in 1912 in the ruins of Gezer, 20 miles (32 km) from Jerusalem. It had been preserved in burned debris that might date from the depredations of Pharaoh Thutmose III, who captured the town and then deported its population to Egypt around 1480 BC.

OLD TESTAMENT PROVERBS INSPIRED BY THE LAND

FROM the diligence of the ant to the process of churning milk to make butter, all kinds of images are used in the Book of Proverbs to castigate idleness, quarrelsomeness and meanness and encourage their opposites such as hard work and generosity:

❛ *Go to the ant, you sluggard; consider its ways and be wise! It has no commander, no overseer or ruler, yet it stores its provisions in summer and gathers its food at harvest.*

I went past the field of the sluggard, past the vineyard of the man who lacks judgment; thorns had come up everywhere, the ground was covered with weeds, and the stone wall was in ruins. I applied my heart to what I observed and learned a lesson from what I saw: A little sleep, a little slumber, a little folding of the hands to rest – and poverty will come on you like a bandit and scarcity like an armed man.

Lazy hands make a man poor, but diligent hands bring wealth.

He who works his land will have abundant food, but he who chases fantasies lacks judgment.

As north wind brings rain, so a sly tongue brings angry looks.

Better a little with the fear of the Lord than great wealth with turmoil.

A generous man will himself be blessed, for he shares his food with the poor.

. . . as churning the milk produces butter, and as twisting the nose produces blood, so stirring up anger produces strife.

In the house of the wise are stores of choice food and oil, but a foolish man devours all he has.

Be sure you know the condition of your flocks, give careful attention to your herds; for riches do not endure for ever, and a crown is not secure for all generations. When the hay is removed and new growth appears and the grass from the hills is gathered in, the lambs will provide you with clothing and the goats with the price of a field. You will have plenty of goats' milk to feed you and your family and to nourish your servant girls. ❜

---

onions and melons. The day's main meal was taken at sunset. To relieve monotonous menus, wives flavoured their boiled stews with garlic, spices and herbs. Although the Israelites had to import some spices from Mesopotamia or even India, they grew the most common herbs themselves – the prophet Isaiah uses the image of the conscientious farmer who scatters dill and sows cumin as well as putting in 'wheat in rows and barley in its proper place'. The Israelites were also lucky enough to have virtually unlimited supplies of salt in the Dead Sea where they gathered it from the shores or the large Hill of Salt at its south-western corner.

Bread and food were interchangeable terms and coarse barley bread was the peasant's staple, baked daily in every home. Grain was sifted in a broad-rimmed basket. Then came the back-breaking task of grinding it into flour with crude millstones. The flour was mixed with salt and water to produce dough; usually this was 'leavened' – raised – with old dough which had fermented.

The simplest method for the traveller was to make dough 'ash cakes' on stones heated by a dung fire and covered with the ashes. Family

ovens consisted of a big upturned earthenware jar with an air vent. The jar was partly sunk in the ground, a fire was set inside and when it died down the women slapped the dough on the hot inner surface via the air vent. The dough stuck there until baked. The dough might be mixed with olive oil or sprinkled with seed. Unleavened dough formed crisp discs that could be sweetened to make honey wafers.

The Book of Samuel includes a record of supplies offered to David and his companions during their days as a guerrilla band: 200 loaves, two skins of wine, five sheep carcasses, five measures of parched grain, 200 bunches of grapes, 200 clusters of raisins and 200 fig cakes. Parched grain consisted of fresh ears lightly roasted; it was a popular snack. Figs preserved by pressing into hard cakes made an ideal packed lunch.

GATHERING THE HARVEST
Men, women and children are all mobilised to reap the harvest, bring it back to the farm on donkeys and store it for the months to come.

A Wine-lover's Guide to the Old Testament

THE ISRAELITES were enthusiastic imbibers, as were most peoples of the ancient Near East. 'How is your wine?' the King of Carchemish wrote to the King of Mari, two friendly potentates along the route of Abraham. 'If you have no decent wine, let me know and I'll send you some.' An Egyptian account has it that wine was more plentiful than water in Canaan. It was certainly safer when cholera, typhoid and dysentery were endemic.

Wine is mentioned almost 200 times in the Bible. It was drunk with meals, during festivals, and for ritual purposes. 'Wine maketh glad the heart of man', sang the Psalmist, and Proverbs recommends it for 'those of heavy heart'. It was available in great variety. There were spiced wines, sweet wines, and bread was dipped in stale wine – vinegar. For everyday purposes wine was mixed with water and in this form it not only raised spirits but also killed dangerous baccili lurking in contaminated water supplies.

Gibeon was a major wine-producing centre near Jerusalem. Scores of underground vats and cellars have been found there capable of storing tens of thousands of

WINE PRESSERS An Egyptian wall painting, from a tomb at Thebes, shows workers treading grapes. The juice runs out into a basin at the right.

QUAFFING VESSELS These bronze vessels, including a wine jug, date from around 1200 BC.

gallons of wine at a constant 18°C (64°F). Gibeon wines from the 7th century BC carried a designation of origin and the name of the vineyard owner on the jar.

The Old Testament has perceptive descriptions of alcoholism: 'Woe unto them that rise up early in the morning, that they may follow strong drink . . . till night.' This 'strong drink' – made from wine grounds, honey and dates – was responsible for the drunkenness which so distressed the prophets.

Beer (or rather ale, since hops would not be added for thousands of years) was most popular in regions where the grape did not flourish, though wine was a major trade item from earliest times.

Mesopotamians quaffed great quantities of beer. Up to 40 per cent of their grain production went to brewers, and the pay for some jobs included 20 pints (11 litres) a day.

The Egyptians took pride in both their beer and wine, as did the Philistines. Travellers judged that Egyptian beer was better than Mesopotamian. Egyptian brews included an extra strong ale with alcoholic content as high as 12 per cent. The Egyptian beers and wines carried exuberant names like 'The Joybringer', 'The Heavenly', 'The Beautiful', 'The Blood-red' and 'Heart's Ease'. Some wine was made for immediate use, but the choicest was sealed in jars or vats and cellared and carried a full provenance: the name of the vineyard, the vintner and the year of growth.

The pharaohs had the pick of the domestic vintage and imported wines; they were partial to the wines from Amurru to the north of Canaan. Lebanon wines, whose fragrance charmed the prophet Hosea, were celebrated throughout the Near East.

MOTHER LOVE A cow suckles her calf in a Phoenician carving from the 8th century BC. Meat-eating became more common as prosperity rose.

The harshest wilderness harboured nourishing opportunities in game and migrant birds. In addition there was 'manna from heaven', a tasty, sticky substance extruded by insects on certain desert plants and locusts were a delicacy favoured by the Assyrians, who served them kebab-style on skewers.

FEASTING ON THE FATTED CALF

Agricultural advances and the benefits flowing from increasing trade brought improvements in diet over time. New seed and grape varieties were introduced and around Jerusalem soil was hauled to the terraced slopes to improve yields. From the 8th century BC, wheat loaves, twice as costly as barley, were being baked in more homes.

The princely set were always a class apart when it came to cuisine. Only the finest wheat flour was good enough for them, and prime venison, while the 'fatted calf' was no figure of speech, but regular fare for the elite. The beasts were stalled in barns ('fattening houses') and fed up before slaughter. The Bible records

FATTENING HOUSE 'Better a meal of vegetables where there is love', says the Book of Proverbs, 'than a fattened calf with hatred.' Veal, unlike vegetables, was rich man's fare.

Solomon's provision list for one day – it included 30 specially pastured and fattened oxen, 100 sheep and more than 1000 bushels of flour and meal.

In excess of 1000 beasts were slaughtered daily for the Persian court, and with reason – the Persian king was accustomed to dining 15 000 guests at a sitting. The cost to his treasury of such a repast was the equivalent of £75 000, but it was no orgy of gluttony. Portions served were modest, and what remained was borne away to feed a multitude of retainers, soldiers and servants.

The royal palate was trained to such a pitch of sensitivity that the king's bread was made of wheat from a Greek island celebrated for the quality of its grain. During dinner, a girl would sing to the accompanying chorus of concubines, some plucking on stringed instruments. Afterwards, royal cronies might be invited to have a drink of wine (though never to share the same wine) with the king, who reclined on his gold-framed couch and sipped from his golden goblet, while they settled around on the carpet. Protocol required them to retire if they got tipsy.

LIFE IN THE CITY

A history of invaders sweeping across the region between Mesopotamia and Egypt

meant that good defences were always a prime consideration for Israelite cities.

In times of peace, the gate was the city's busy focal point.

AN ISRAELITE CITY was a romantic sight, from a distance. Like a fairy castle, it seemed to perch perilously on a hilltop, threatening to topple over but for the stout girdling wall that held it together.

The wall described a wobbly circle, dipping and swaying in response to the contours of the hill. No work of art, it was a mixture of stone and mud brick, patched and buttressed and patched again, and telling a tale of centuries of sack and renewal. It was impressive most of all for its bulk, as much as 30 ft (9 m) thick and rising 50 ft (15 m) or more, or as Deuteronomy poetically puts it, 'fenced up to heaven'.

Within the wall there was hardly room to breathe, so excess habitation spilled out and down the slope, sometimes to be protected by a second, outer wall. The hill itself was a living thing. Part natural, part midden, it was an ever-swelling mound gorging upon the debris of generations of endeavour.

In Egypt the needs of farming the rich river soil deposited by the Nile provided the impetus for large communities to come together in towns or cities, but in the minds of the peoples across the sands of Sinai defence was always uppermost. Some 2000 years before the Israelites, the Egyptians described the early cities of Canaan as 'fortified enclosures'. Many millennia before this, the earliest town that archaeologists have so far excavated, Jericho, had a sturdy 12 ft (3.7 m) stone wall to protect a population of perhaps 2000.

For 7000 years, the wall-builders fought a losing technological battle against the wall-scalers. No matter how big or broad the fortifications, invaders found a way over, through, or under them. Over the centuries, city mounds were bolstered at their top with landfill from ditches dug at their base, and walls were fronted with sloping, slippery ramps which sent chariots and later the newfangled battering rams and siege towers slithering backwards. But for each defensive advance there was a corresponding advance in assault tactics.

CLAMOUR AT THE GATE

Civilisation in more secure or expansive locations evolved an urban environment worthy of the name. Mesopotamian cities sprawling across their plain were huge, as was Memphis in Egypt where rich people had homes set in tree-shaded gardens with

GOING INTO EXILE The inhabitants of a vanquished city – possibly Biblical Ashtaroth, lying to the east of the Jordan – carry their possessions on their shoulders as they are led off by their Assyrian conquerors.

ASSYRIAN ASSAULT A relief from the royal palace at Nineveh shows a battering ram being driven against a wall during Sennacherib's siege of Lachish, an important fortified city in Judah, in 587-586 BC.

private lakes. In the Canaanite highlands, whose narrow valleys were strategic routes for trade and war, there was neither time nor room for anything that smacked of luxury.

City in a real sense was an inappropriate word for the hilltop keeps which went by that name, acting as administrative centres for surrounding populations of farmers or pastoralists living in villages and hamlets. They rarely amounted to more than a few cramped acres, and the only open space was by the city gate. This made the gate the noisy hub of urban life, and here the elders – patriarchs of the leading families – sat on benches to dispense justice and run local government.

Every sort and condition of society thronged the gate, which was London's Oxford Street and Soho, Horse Guards' Parade and the Old Bailey all on one spot. Here was the produce market, and the stalls of traders in pretty ribbons and Egyptian jewellery, Arabian perfumes and Phoenician furniture,

BEYOND THE WALL   A man selling land gives his sandal to the buyer to show he has given up his right to the land.

FORMED IN CLAY The potter bending over his wheel in his workshop was a familiar sight of the cities. These Israelite pitchers date from the 6th century BC.

Home furniture was basic. A bed, a table, a stool and a lamp were facilities accorded a distinguished guest. Most people slept on a straw mat or a rug, wrapped in the cloak they wore by day. Meals were taken squatting. Utensils were simple, and customarily of clay: metal was expensive.

The discomforts of a leaky Israelite house in the cold and damp of winter are conveyed in a maxim from the Book of Proverbs: 'A nagging woman is like the drip, drip, drip on a rainy day.' If a home had a fireplace it was a hole dug in the floor where dung cakes smouldered and, without a chimney to draw off the fumes, the effect could be suffocating.

Summer sizzle was evidently more distressing than winter chill for, where possible, houses were built facing north. On hot nights, families could repair to the flat roof for a comfortable night's sleep. Here they could take the air, chat with the neighbours, or visit them, since gaps between houses were narrow enough to stride across. To 'proclaim from the housetops' was to make a public announcement, and roof altars to dubious gods were common enough to disgust the purist prophets. The roof was also a convenient workplace, where flax could be dried, and washing too. Accidents were so frequent that a law eventually required new home builders to surround the roof with a parapet to prevent people falling off.

copper ingots and daggers of iron. It is not hard to imagine the din of the hawkers, the whine of beggars, scribes touting for business, labourers seeking a day's hire and litigants loudly arguing a case. And all the while old acquaintances were stepping gingerly through the muck and jostle, striving to be heard as they exchanged the elaborate, formal greetings which everyone so delighted in.

Completing the chaos were the arrivals and departures of caravans – bearers of news as well as goods – and the occasional stark drama of an execution by stoning, a participatory event in which 'all the men of the city' were encouraged to lend a hand.

CITY HOUSING

Within the city, space was at a premium. Single-file alleyways along which a loaded pack-donkey could hardly squeeze wound between the walls of tightly packed homes. Walls were mostly of mudbrick bonded with clay and set on a rough-hewn stone foundation. The flimsy flat roofs of clay over brushwood had to be tamped down with a kind of garden roller after a downpour.

Homes had tiny windows only, partly for ease of construction, but also to thwart the hot summer sun, and no more than the dim, olive-oil flicker of a tiny clay lamp to pierce the gloom. By necessity as much as preference, the Israelites were an outdoor people.

LIVING WITHOUT PLUMBING

Sanitation did not exist, except at the crudest level, as in the prophet Jeremiah's description of dead donkeys being dragged forth and thrown outside the gate of Jerusalem. Human waste might be deposited in nearby fields, or in communal dung heaps, but there is little evidence of organised refuse collection and much must have been left to the scavenging of dogs, jackals or birds.

The better palaces of the Near East had piped water and the best-appointed homes had an indoor toilet set against an outside wall. In Egypt and Mesopotamia, the hot sun quickly dried and detoxified ordure, but with their variable weather the urban Israelites were not so fortunate. Because their cities were so cramped, they also lacked the amenity of an urban orchard or green glade, which in those other lands was a sanitary as well as scenic asset.

Once the city gate was slammed shut for the night, noise would slowly die down, to be broken only by yapping dogs and the occasional cry of a nightwatchman. With dawn, a great throng burst forth at the opening of the gate, for the daily commute was away from the city, which is why the

NIGHT LIGHT Pottery lamps like this were filled with oil – usually olive oil or animal fat – and had a wick made of flax or a piece of rag.

Biblical Psalmist sang of 'going out and coming in', in that order. The separation of town and country as we know it hardly existed, and even in winter townsfolk went out daily to tend the surrounding crops and flocks. In summer, so long as no enemy threatened, a city might be quite deserted during the daylight hours.

WATER EMERGENCIES

However excellent its defences, any city's capacity to endure siege was dependent upon its food and water reserves. In 1486 BC an Egyptian army arrived outside Megiddo, 20 miles (32 km) from modern Haifa, in time to reap for itself the grain harvest – 450 000 bushels were recorded by the pharaoh's scribes – and the city was starved into surrender in seven months.

Cisterns held a water supply replenished by the muddy, murky run-off from chance rainfall, but

---

EYEWITNESS

TWO SPIES AND A PROSTITUTE

THE STREETS of Jericho are the setting for a Biblical episode mingling espionage and prostitution. Spies were sent ahead by Moses' successor Joshua as the Israelites made their first cautious approach to the 'promised land':

❛ Then Joshua son of Nun secretly sent two spies from Shittim. "Go, look over the land," he said, "especially Jericho." So they went and entered the house of a prostitute named Rahab and stayed there.

The king of Jericho was told, "Look! Some of the Israelites have come here tonight to spy out the land." So the king of Jericho sent this message to Rahab: "Bring out the men who . . . entered your house, because they have come to spy out the whole land."

But the woman had taken the two men and hidden them. She said, "Yes, the men came to me, but I did not know where they had come from. At dusk, when it was time to close the city gate, the men left. I don't know which way they went. Go after them quickly. . . ." (But she had taken them up to the roof and hidden them under the stalks of flax she had laid out on the roof.) So the men set out in pursuit . . . , and as soon as [they] had gone out, the gate was shut.

Before the spies lay down for the night, she went up on the roof and said to them, "I know that the Lord has given this land to you and that a great fear of you has fallen on us. . . . Now then, please swear to me by the Lord that you will show kindness to my family, because I have shown kindness to you. . . ."

"Our lives for your lives!" the men assured her. "If you don't tell what we are doing, we will treat you kindly and faithfully when the Lord gives us the land."

So she let them down by a rope through the window, for the house she lived in was part of the city wall. Now she had said to them, "Go to the hills so that the pursuers will not find you. Hide yourselves there three days until they return, and then go on your way." ❜

ROOFTOP LIVING The flat roof was an important part of the
home where people ate, worked and sometimes slept.

THE ISRAELITES AT HOME

THE ISRAELITES did not have the technology to build high – a single upper floor was about the limit – so ground space was the measure of affluence. Where possible, a hollow square was the most popular house layout. Living quarters were at the rear of an enclosed courtyard, faced on two sides by rooms used partly or wholly for storing grain, oil and wine. A subterranean water-cistern to collect rainwater was a valued feature and,

in the best appointed homes a stone stairway led to the roof, but ordinary folk made do with a stepladder.

Stone was plentiful but not the tools for cutting and dressing it, so mudbrick was commonly used in home construction, usually reinforced with chopped straw, which released acid compounds that increased the binding effect.

Sometimes fragments of pottery and stone chips were added to the mix. These bricks were larger than

their modern counterparts and were rugged enough to serve in fortifications.

Structural engineering was basic, and windows were of necessity usually tiny slits. The puritanical prophets found virtue in such limitations and protested at the growing affluence of their times, roundly condemning those able to indulge in 'houses of hewn stones' or to make their homes 'wide' with 'cut-out windows'.

otherwise the inhabitants of a besieged city were caught high and dry. Some of the greatest engineering works of the age were enterprises of desperation – secret tunnels dug down to the base-rock and out beyond the mound to the nearest source of fresh water.

The water tunnels of Jerusalem are the best known, though there were similar ones at the important fort-cities of Megiddo and Hazor in the north. The first shaft at Jerusalem was dug through the rock under the city wall to the Gihon Spring (now the Virgin's Fountain) in Canaanite times, and this may be how David's intrepid commandos crept up and captured the little city around 1000 BC. Three centuries later, when the Assyrians were threatening Judah, a much improved system delivering a constant water supply was devised under King Hezekiah. It incorporated a roomy 1750 ft (533 m) tunnel feeding an underground cistern.

Gangs of miners dug from either end, feeling

their way by guesswork and taking advantage of natural fissures, until one side heard the pickaxes of the other and made the necessary correction in direction to break through. This achievement merited a mention in the Bible.

ARCHITECTURAL LIMITATIONS

Construction everywhere was limited by the raw materials at hand. From Sumer to Babylon, the magnificence of Mesopotamian civilisation was built upon river mud, baked by the hot sun into brick. For reinforcement and waterproofing, people had dried reeds and bitumen, the tarry substance oozing from unsuspected oil fields that would fuel an unimaginable future world.

The fortunate Egyptians were walled in by sand and limestone, building-blocks for their monuments. Canaan had its chalky, rocky hillsides, and mudbrick where rock was less accessible; the rock was soft, and slabs obligingly bonded as they hardened with exposure to the air. For the finishing touch to grand enterprises, builders turned to the prized wood of the Lebanon range, 'the Mountain of Cedars'.

The Israelites had no architectural tradition of their own. For his building projects Solomon hired Phoenician craftsmen from Tyre, just then getting into its stride as a booming port and culture mart, and adopted the best in Canaanite style, augmented

continued on page 42

EVERYDAY SIGHT
The donkey was the most widely used pack animal – as in this clay model – while both rich and poor also used it to ride on.

WATER SUPPLY   King Hezekiah's water tunnel, which was built before 701 BC, was an impressive feat of engineering that involved boring through the rock from both sides and meeting in the middle.

LIFE AT THE CITY GATES

Traders have taken advantage of the open space at the city gates to set up their stalls. The wealthy ride past in their chariots; humbler folk lead pack-donkeys. In peacetime, the gates were the city's most important meeting place where people gathered to bring cases before the city elders, discuss business, make deals or just chat.

In times of war, the gates' different layers of defences came into their own. These included two closely guarded narrow gateways positioned at right angles to one another and a series of stoutly built towers set into the walls. The outer gateway was reached up a steep ramp. At night, even in peacetime, the gates were shut and barred.

by ideas brought across the Mediterranean by the Philistines. There may even have been a national plan, with the same blueprint for an improved city gate employed in several places – Megiddo, Hazor, Gezer, Shechem and Tirzah. These gates were elaborate multistorey structures and easily the grandest city feature.

At Megiddo, an outer gate led to a fortified courtyard that exposed any unwelcome visitors to a concentrated fire of arrows from above. At the head of the courtyard loomed the main gate, fronted by two great doors of hardened, metal-hinged cypress and backed by three further entryways, one after the other, with recesses for defenders at each stage. Above the gate was a chamber, and above this a lookout post.

Another key development was the casemate, or hollow city wall. Cheaper and quicker to build than the solid version, the casemate gave nothing away in breadth, while it had the advantage of providing premium space for constructing warehouses and shops within the walls.

URBAN IMPROVEMENTS

Royal needs took precedence. At the time of its completion the royal compound occupied almost half of Jerusalem, then a modest 32 acres (13 ha), and most of the city's few thousand inhabitants must have been directly or indirectly employed in court service. The Bible states that building Solomon's temple took seven years but, true to princely priorities, the adjoining palace complex took twice as long.

JERICHO – A WORLD WAITING TO BE REVEALED

THE BIBLE relates how Joshua laid siege to Jericho. For six days his troops, led by priests blowing rams' horns, marched around its walls. On their seventh circuit of the seventh day the Israelites let out a shout, and the walls came tumbling down. Archaeologists have failed to find confirming evidence of the Biblical story, but they have laid bare one of the longest-running records of habitation anywhere on earth.

Slicing into a *tell*, a man-made mound created by centuries of settlement, opens a storybook whose pages are its layered debris, providing a chronological history pushing back further in time the deeper you delve. Jericho's is the oldest book of all. Seventy feet (21 m) down, at bedrock, diggers found floors for rounded huts or tents and flint tools

LAYERED CITY An aerial photograph shows excavations under way on a *tell*. On the left is the trench where the excavations have sliced through its many layers.

of the people who first settled this choice spot, kept green and fertile by a stream bubbling from the base of the Judaean hills. Through scraps of charred wood they were able to carbon-date the settlement to about 7800 BC.

Some 13 ft (4 m) above bedrock and dated 1000 years later, the diggers had previously come upon one of the world's earliest-known cities. Its most remarkable feature was a

round tower of stone, still preserved to a height of 30 ft (9 m). Built 5000 years before the pyramids, it is the earliest stone building of any size so far discovered.

Jerichoans of 6000 BC had greeted the diggers at a higher level – their skulls restored to living likeness with a sculpting of painted plaster. Sifting through the debris the archaeologists pieced together the lives of a community growing grain and trading in the resources of the Dead Sea – salt, sulphur, bitumen. Above the skull people, the fortifications grew stronger, the pots and tools more sophisticated.

Jericho's walls had tumbled – often. In one 1000-year period they had been repaired or rebuilt 16 times and there were several fiery destructions, though none that could be dated to the Israelites.

HOUSEHOLD FURNISHINGS Servants carry in tables and a bowl of food for the king in an Assyrian relief of the 8th century BC. Clay models found at Lachish show Israelite styles of furniture between the 10th and 8th centuries BC.

Solomon's excesses were followed by revolution and a permanent division between the kingdoms of Judah and Israel, but urban development still gathered pace. Israel, bereft of Jerusalem, eventually built a new capital, Samaria. Judah, despite its midget dimensions, also prospered and Jerusalem quadrupled in size over the next 250 years.

Archaeologists digging up early 7th-century BC Beersheba, lying in the far south of Judah on the edge of the Negev desert, found a well-laid-out town of 25 acres (10 ha) that eliminated some of the congestion and chaos of the past. A sturdy three-stage gate led directly into an open market area with adjacent storehouses. From this core, concentric street-paths ran round the oval interior of the town like a swiss roll.

An improved 'Israelite' house style was well established by the 8th century BC. For this, the home was constructed around three sides of an open courtyard, with a retaining wall providing privacy along the fourth side and punctuated by a modest doorway letting onto the street or alleyway. Stones were much better trimmed than before and corners well bonded.

More wood was incorporated into structures and furniture improved – low, wide chairs and couches with loose covers came into vogue among the wealthy classes. Upper storeys became more common, as did summer parlours – 'upper chambers of cooling', as their name translates in the

The City Where the Small Are Like the Great

Egyptian cities, with their gardens, orchards and surrounding fields, were some of the finest in the Near East. Here a scribe extolls the beauties of Raamses, the very city, according to the Bible, on which the children of Israel laboured while still enslaved by the Egyptians:

❛ The [city] is pleasant in life; . . . it is full of supplies and food every day, its ponds with fish, and its lakes with birds. Its meadows are verdant with grass; its banks bear dates; its melons are abundant on the sands . . . Its granaries are so full of barley and emmer [a kind of wheat] that they come near to the sky. Onions and leeks are for food, and lettuce of the garden, pomegranates, apples and olives, figs of the orchard, sweet wine of Ka-of-Egypt, surpassing honey, red *wedj* fish . . . , which live on lotus flowers, *bedin* fish of the Hari-waters, . . .

Its ships go out and come back to mooring, so that supplies and food are in it every day. One rejoices to dwell within it, and none says: "Would that!" to it. The small in it are like the great. ❜

---

original Hebrew. Lacking window glass, these posed a hazard, as is evident from the fate of King Ahaziah, who in 849 BC 'fell down through the lattice of his upper chamber . . . and was sick'.

The effects of social stratification became apparent, with the well-to-do able to afford larger homes which tended to be built on the western edge of the mound, where the prevailing west wind brought some relief and blew away foul odours. The poor, where not pushed out of the city altogether, crammed into shacks pulled together from the remains of previous structures.

MODEL CITIES – DASHED DREAMS

Fundamental needs did not alter with time. In siting a new city, the prime considerations were its defensibility and close proximity to a spring or other adequate water supply, together with access to an agricultural area and a trade route.

The most ardent urban planner of the age was the Assyrian king and conqueror Sennacherib, and numbers of Israelite captives must have laboured at his great creation, the model city of Nineveh. Early in the 7th century BC Sennacherib had become disenchanted with the old city on the upper Tigris and had determined on a complete rebuilding to incorporate the latest ideas in open-plan living.

He doubled Nineveh's size by building a 15 gate enclosure wall more than 6 miles (9 km) in circumference. He enlarged squares, straightened and widened streets, and pulled down buildings to improve access and light. He allotted citizens 2 acre (0.8 ha) orchard plots and created a wildlife park with imported trees, aromatic plants and cotton bushes to support a weaving industry. To supplement river water, clear mountain streams were tapped and diverted 30 miles (48 km) by canal and aqueduct. For himself, Sennacherib replaced the existing palace (it was pokey and 'in poor taste', he explained) with a splendid new one.

A further outer wall and a 50 yd (46 m) moat, looped into the Tigris, provided Nineveh with state-of-the art defences, but to no avail. Before the century was out, Sennacherib's model metropolis was overrun and destroyed by the Babylonians. Likewise Jerusalem: of its Old Testament glories only the Bible can speak, for by 586 BC it had been reduced by Babylonian conquerors to a ramshackle shell.

Its very insecurity as a sanctuary made an Old Testament city the soul of the age, a place for which its inhabitants felt very deeply. The Song of Solomon associates this attachment with that for a lover: 'Thou art beautiful as Tirzah, my love, comely as Jerusalem.' Long before, a poet lamented one of Ur's destructions.

My palm groves and vineyards once abundant
*   in honey and wine are tangled with thorns.*
My bare plain is parched like an oven.
My river is clogged with waterweed.
My chariot road sprouts mountain thorn.
The very bricks cry out with a human voice:
*   'Where, pray?'*

. . . and 431 further lines of anguish.

FAMILY LIFE IN BIBLE TIMES

The family, the extended family or clan and the tribe were the building-blocks of
Israelite society. Families worked together, lived together, clung together for
all-important mutual support. Fathers taught their sons their trades; girls
learned the skills of domestic management. Even relatively modest households
owned some slaves. Although prophets railed increasingly against the luxurious
excesses of the rich, for most ordinary people their homes remained simple.

A Society of Patriarchs

The successful patriarch headed a large and ever-growing household with a full

complement of wives, children, children-in-law, grandchildren and slaves. Within this

community every member had a part to play in ensuring the family's prosperity.

OLD TESTAMENT LIFE was, for the majority of people, hazardous and short. A glance at the Hebrew Bible – the Old Testament – reveals the often random violence of war, while the constant threat of plague, pestilence, uncertain rains and untrustworthy neighbours made anyone's future problematic. In these circumstances, and at a time when disease was commonly considered to be a punishment of the gods or the work of evil spirits, making it through to old age brought respect as nothing else could. While a coddled pharaoh of Egypt or a Persian potentate might attain 'the fullness of years', a peasant was doing well to reach 40.

The Israelites carving out their little state in the backhills of the Mediterranean's eastern shore drew strength in this respect from the wonderful tales of their origins. According to these, the ten generations from Adam through to Noah were said to have lived a combined 8575 years. Even Abraham, a much closer forebear, was credited with 175 highly active years and Moses was said to have been keen-eyed and virile to the last, at 120.

According to Exodus, Moses led the Israelites to their Promised Land where succeeding generations

IN THE BEGINNING

The word 'Bible' derives from Byblos, a Phoenician port north of Beirut, and from the Greek word for papyrus, a reed used for making sails, rope and paper for writing-scrolls. Byblos was such a heavy user of papyrus, and trader in it, that the product became associated with the city. Books in Greek were consequently known as *biblia*, hence Bible . . . The Book.

established themselves as settled farmers – but only just, their hold on the land no deeper than the grit in their fingernails. Desert-dictated rules of survival, dating from their earlier, purely nomadic existence, remained deeply ingrained. In the desert, solitary survival was impossible: the family was the only practical unit of existence. Families bonded tightly into extended families, or clans, sharing the name of a valiant ancestor, such as the clan of the Abiezrites to which the reforming leader Gideon belonged. Clans were grouped into tribes – the Abiezrites were part of the tribe of Manasseh – with shifting, wary alliances tied to grazing and water rights.

ON THE MOVE Clans of nomads moved from place to place taking their flocks and belongings with them. Many made their way to Egypt, sometimes to trade, sometimes hoping to settle there in periods of drought.

UR OF THE CHALDEES The founding Biblical patriarch Abraham set out from Ur, one of the world's first cities, on the banks of the Euphrates. In the background here are the remains of one of its temple towers or ziggurats.

For each family, procreation was a high priority if it was to thrive and multiply. There was no word for bachelor in the Hebrew language and marrying early was the manly thing to do. 'As arrows in the hand of a mighty man, so are the children of one's youth,' sang the Biblical psalmist. 'Happy is that man that hath his quiver full of them.' The average youth could expect to become a father before he was 20, a grandfather in his thirties, and a great-grandfather by his fifties.

In theory at least, landed property belonged to the family as a whole, never to individuals, and a family's right to its land was supposed to be inalienable. But as societies became more sophisticated the consolidation of land in fewer hands became a constant problem as richer families bypassed the rules to buy up the lands of poorer neighbours.

A number of Near Eastern cultures tried to protect heirs with laws limiting the transfer or sale of land to a nearest relative, but by the middle of the 2nd millennium BC the Mesopotamians in particular had found a way around this. The landowner simply legalised a sale by 'adopting' the purchaser for the purposes of the transaction.

BE FRUITFUL AND MULTIPLY

The Israelites experienced many upheavals after consolidating as a people late in the 2nd millennium BC. They stayed united through much of the 10th century BC under the rule of King David and King Solomon, only to split permanently into bickering and sometimes warring northern and southern kingdoms, Israel and Judah.

Picked off by powerful invaders, notably the Assyrians and Babylonians, they had lost even Jerusalem by the early 6th century BC. Then a half-century forced exile of their aristocracy in Babylon was followed by colonial rule under the Persians and, after them, the Greeks. All this caused changes in attitude and outlook yet, throughout

WEATHER GOD
Most families had figurines of their gods. The Canaanite god Baal was one of these.

1000 years of fluctuating fortunes, up to 90 per cent of the people remained rooted to the land, with farming family households as the basic unit of society.

These households were self-contained, labour-intensive enterprises wresting a living out of the hillsides, and having to produce by their own efforts everything they needed for survival. The Biblical injunction to 'be fruitful and multiply' made compelling sense in such circumstances, since a large family made for a more viable operation.

The ideal family was the ideal workforce: a multi-generational combine of kin, close knit by blood and marriage. Typically, there would be a senior couple residing with their sons and unmarried daughters, their sons' spouses and children, the odd orphaned niece, nephew and widowed sibling, and whatever slaves they might have accumulated. Each was a dynamic community in constant flux.

A village was organised into family clusters, each cluster centred upon the household of the oldest active male member, who was leader and lord of his extended family. Upon his death or

CHANGE AND CONTINUITY An Assyrian relief shows Jehu King of Israel paying homage to Shalmaneser of Assyria. Kings and conquerors came and went, but for most ordinary people, family life carried on its age-old traditions.

disablement, there would be a swift rearrangement around the immediate family of his senior son.

Peace and harmony were hard to sustain, since these large groups provided ample opportunity for tension and disagreement. The early books of the Bible abound in evidence of this, some of their most compelling tales being concerned with family jealousy and fratricidal rivalry. The friction resulting from favouritism and competing claims for attention – as in the story of the patriarch Isaac's sons, Esau and Jacob – is the stuff of a number of crucial Biblical plots.

THE WANDERER'S LIFE
To survive in the desert, families and clans had to bond together tightly.

49

THE ADVENTURES OF AN EGYPTIAN 'ABRAHAM'

AN ACCOUNT of the kind of life led by the Biblical patriarchs was written by an Egyptian political refugee whose adventures took him along much the same path as Abraham, only in the opposite direction – from the lands around the Nile up into the hill country of Canaan. His story was immensely popular with generations of Egyptians and has survived the centuries.

Sinuhe was a courtier who feared being implicated in a palace conspiracy. In early March 1960 BC he fled in the night. Avoiding populated areas, he crossed the Nile near the site of modern Cairo and

FATAL WEAPON A 9th-century BC relief shows a warrior firing a sling shot of the kind that David would have used to fell Goliath.

slipped past the guards manning border fortifications.

Trudging eastward into Sinai, he was soon near to collapse from thirst and panic. 'This is the taste of death', he thought, but the sounds of livestock led him to a band of nomads. They gave him food and water. Passing from tribe to tribe through the Canaan hill country, he reached the northern highlands. A local ruler welcomed the sophisticated wanderer as a teacher to his children. He married Sinuhe to his eldest daughter and then gave him his pick of territory and retainers. Sinuhe prospered.

He gained a reputation as a generous host. He also became a military adviser, then commander of the ruler's forces: 'Every tribe against which I went forth was driven from its pastures and its wells. I plundered its cattle, [and] carried off its inhabitants, . . .'

His boldest adventure anticipated the Biblical story of David and Goliath. As he described it, a 'mighty man', the supreme warrior in all Canaan, challenged him to single combat. Sinuhe reasoned that he was resented for his success as 'a stray bull in the herd'. He accepted the challenge: 'The night before the fight, I polished my weapons and strung my bow, practised archery and played with my dagger.

When day broke, a good half of Canaan had gathered. Every heart burned for me; . . .'

The Canaanite warrior strode forward with shield, battle-axe and an armful of javelins which he proceeded to pitch at the Egyptian upstart, who managed to evade them. Then: 'He charged me, and I shot him, my arrow sticking in his neck. He bellowed loudly and fell on his nose. I seized his battle-axe and killed him with it, and raised my cry of victory over his body while everybody roared.' Sinuhe gave praise to Montu, the Egyptian god of war. Then he plundered the fallen champion's encampment and rounded up his livestock.

But Sinuhe was homesick as only an Egyptian could be. His former employer, the Princess Nefru, was now queen and the royal children wrote to him. He was enticed home with promises of the ultimate reward to which a pharaoh's man could aspire. When the time came, he would have the kind of top-class funeral and mummification that guaranteed eternal life.

So Sinuhe handed over to his eldest son 'my tribe and all my property . . . ; my serfs, all my animals, my fruit trees'. Welcomed back, he lived 'under the favour of the king's presence until the day of mooring [death] had come'.

Family and community stability rested on the authority of the father, the head of the household. Parents might even have an unruly son put to death. As Deuteronomy chillingly laid down: 'If a man has a stubborn and rebellious son who does not obey his father and mother and will not listen to them when they discipline him, his father and mother shall take hold of him and bring him to the elders at the gate of his town. They shall say to the elders: "This son

of ours is stubborn and rebellious. He will not obey us. He is a profligate and a drunkard." Then all the men of his town shall stone him to death.'

POWER IN A NAME
All names were personal. Surnames in the modern sense were not used. Instead men were known as, say, Manasseh son of Hezekiah – since the family connection was so dominant it needed no further

emphasising. Choosing a child's personal name, however, was a serious matter, as it was believed to be invested with powers which could effect one's destiny.

Commonly throughout the Near East a person's name would incorporate the name of a god, making it a kind of talisman, or protective prayer. Nathaniel and well over 100 other Biblical names contain, for example, the compound 'el'. El was the supreme god of the Canaanites and came to stand for deities in general including the God of Israel. Joshua, meaning 'God is salvation', similarly invokes Yahweh, protective deity of the Israelites. Isaiah means 'Yahweh is salvation'; Elijah, a combination of El and Yahweh, could be directly translated as 'Yahweh is my God' or 'Yahweh saves'.

Not all names had such portentious meanings. Sometimes they referred to the circumstances of the baby's birth, or pointed to some characteristic, or reflected the family's hopes or feelings at the time. Names might be changed later to try to alter a person's destiny for the better, a Biblical example being the name-change from Ben-oni ('son of my sorrow') to Benjamin, ('son of my right hand'). Names like Deborah (bee), Rachel (ewe) or Caleb (dog) were intended to invoke the best attributes of their namesakes, though Leah (wild cow) loses a lot in its modern context and it is hard to see

INVADERS FROM BEYOND War and invasion were a constant threat. These men are Assyrians whose nation destroyed the northern kingdom of Israel in 722-721 BC.

how Esau (hairy) or Gareb (scabby) took pride in such epithets.

A child's upbringing was rigorous from the very first moment, when the newborn infant was rubbed with salt, possibly as a protection from evil spirits,

INTO BONDAGE Captives from Lachish in Judah are driven into exile by their Assyrian conquerors. Usually the nobles only were picked out for exile.

SEALED UP Two seals and a bulla, a seal's impression in clay belonged (left to right) to Saul son of Elisha; Pedaiah, a prince of Judah; and Gemariah son of Shaphan, a scribe mentioned by the prophet Jeremiah.

who were considered to be particularly pernicious. Once they were eight days old, Israelite boys were circumcised in a ritual operation performed with a flint knife. Circumcision was also practised by the Egyptians and a number of other Near Eastern peoples. Its origins are lost, but to the Israelites it became an all-important badge of identity that was symbolic of the special relationship or covenant between them and their God.

Babies were nursed at the breast longer than is usual today – for two years or more – and as toddlers they remained in the care of their mothers. Girls stayed with their mothers throughout childhood learning domestic skills such as spinning, weaving and baking. Boys were soon placed under the discipline of fathers who were under stern injunction not to spare the rod. As the Book of Proverbs puts it: 'Do not withhold discipline from a child; if you punish him with the rod, he will not die. Punish him with the rod and save his soul from death.'

Advice this stern was not wholeheartedly followed, however, and there is ample evidence of sons being spoiled. Even so, disobedience to either parent was a disgrace to family and community alike. A son who struck his father could have his hand amputated in the Babylon of Abraham's day.

FOLLOWING FATHER'S FOOTSTEPS

The principle that a son should take up his father's occupation was as deeply rooted as patriarchy in the ancient Near East. From a very early age Israelite boys commenced on-the-job training with their fathers. Those not committed to farming

---

EYEWITNESS

'OTHER BOYS HELP TO SUPPORT THEIR PARENTS'

PUPILS toiling in the schools of Ur and other Mesopotamian cities had strikingly familiar concerns: how to play truant and avoid a caning from their teacher, their father, or both. Their brick benches and clay tablet 'exercise books' have been unearthed and so have details of their daily lives, even their conversations, such as this exchange between a father and his malingering son:

❝ *Where have you been?*
'I haven't been anywhere.'
'If you haven't been anywhere,
why are you loafing around?

Get to school! Don't hang about in the public square; don't wander the streets. Be a man! Night and day you give me heartache; night and day you play around. Other boys help to support their parents. I've never even made you plough my field. You – you're only a man when it comes to perversity. I'm furious with you!'

The story of one boy's school-day started as it might today:

'I got up early in the morning. My mother gave me two rolls and I set off for school.'

He arrived late, and got caned. He was caned again for talking, then for a botched essay. But this lad had an indulgent father who invited the schoolmaster home, plied him with food and wine, gave him a new gown and other presents and then had his son go through his exercises before the much-mollified guest. The ploy worked, for the anecdote ends with his teacher telling the boy:

'Young man, because you have heeded my words I believe you can become top in your class – best in the whole school. You will go far! ❞

FAMILY AS WORK FORCE Every member of a potter's family helps out, from the children preparing the lumps of clay to the person heaving pots into the kiln. The pitcher (left) was made by a Philistine potter of the 12th century BC.

learned their father's craft. A few children, like the prophet Samuel when he was a small boy, were handed over to the care of priests who gave them a more formal schooling.

Literacy came to be fairly widespread among the Israelites, certainly the upper classes who may have been taught, like Samuel, by priests. In the Book of Judges the leader Gideon captures a young man from Succoth, a city that has proved itself less than friendly to him. Gideon questions the man who, without any apparent difficulty, writes down a list of 77 elders of Succoth – whom Gideon will later punish by beating them 'with desert thorns and briers'.

Israelite parents were supposed to give their children a sound religious grounding, keeping alive the traditional accounts of Yahweh's dealings with their nation as well as moral teachings. The book of Deuteronomy is clear on the subject: 'Only be careful, and watch yourselves closely so that you do not forget the things your eyes have seen or let them slip from your heart as long as you live. Teach them to your children and to their children after them.'

Education and training among other Near Eastern peoples was in many ways similar. Among the Babylonians, the gods decreed that a man should follow in his father's footsteps, so that it was not only likely but religiously correct for the son of a carpenter or sheep shearer, mat-maker or canal-digger to take up his father's calling, generation after generation. Apprenticeships in Babylon lasted as long as six years.

In these urban civilisations of Mesopotamia, a formal education was the key to higher success. Traditions of scholarship were inculcated using an education system whose stern spirit and methods of teaching by rote had much in common with that of Victorian England. Pupils attended the 'tablet house' – school – from sunrise to sunset, from early youth to maturity. Slackers got the cane.

In the Mesopotamian city of Ur students had only three days a month free, plus three on which they were obliged to attend religious festivals. The curriculum ranged from arithmetic to astronomy, and consisted of constant copying exercises, with little or no opportunity for creative interpretation. Graduation guaranteed a place among the privileged, with assured careers in temple or government, or

WHAT'S IN A NAME?

The Assyrian king Tiglath-pileser III is called 'Pul' in the Bible. Assyrian and Babylonian monarchs had personal names by which they were familiarly known, as well as the formal 'throne names' that have come down to us on tablets and inscriptions. Nebuchadnezzar, for example, translates as 'O god Nebo, protect my frontier-markers'. His off-duty name is not known.

in private practice as scribes serving the needs of the illiterate majority.

In similarly bureaucratic Egypt schoolboy texts exalted the status of the scribe. The names of famous scribes from the past 'are still pronounced because of their books which they made', observes one fragment dating from around 1300 BC. 'A man is perished, his corpse is dust, all his relatives are come to the ground – but it is writing that makes him remembered in the mouth of a reciter.'

MARTIAL CULTURES

The Assyrians cultivated warlike qualities in their young. As soon as he could walk, an Assyrian of good birth was taught to ride and use a bow. Some time before the age of ten, he was put in the charge of a priest or scribe to have the elements of writing drummed into him. But for him education was not as important as connections. The right word – and gift – in the right quarter and the youth might be appointed a page at court, the first rung on the ladder of Assyrian public service.

By his late teens, an aspiring soldier-courtier could expect to accompany the king on campaign, running alongside the royal chariot and helping to haul it over

IN SACRED MEMORY An Israelite father introduces his sons to the rites of the Passover festival. He is using a sprig of marjoram to daub the blood of a sacrificial lamb above the doorway of their home.

ARCHERS OF ASSYRIA **The education of young Assyrian nobles included a substantial period of military service.**

rough ground. This led to a commission as a junior officer, command of a unit and, if all went well, command of an outpost. This in turn carried responsibility for regional security and tax collection, which consisted of overseeing the dispatch of grain and livestock tribute to the cities of the empire. Success in a series of administrative posts led to a provincial governorship and then a career-capping officiating role at the New Year festival in the capital.

An Assyrian male married in his early teens – his parents arranged the match. Despite monogamy being at some periods in Assyrian history the

KING OF KINGS **Illiteracy did not prevent Darius I of Persia from building a huge empire.**

rule, there was nothing to stop him from stocking his home with female captives who doubled as servants for his wife and concubines for himself.

Among the Persians, the martial tradition went deeper still. The three essentials required of a well-bred boy were to ride well, handle a bow skilfully and have the habit of speaking truthfully. A boy was taken from his mother in childhood and placed with foster parents, the better to knock sentiment out of him. Around the age of 15, those selected as *kardakes*, professional soldiers, went to training schools in which they lived in platoons of 50.

The Persian king Darius the Great could neither read nor write. But this evidently held no disadvantage in his mind, judging by the jaunty confidence of his self-description: 'Trained am I, both with hand and feet. As a horseman, I am a good horseman. As a bowman, I am a good bowman, both on foot and on horseback. As a spearman, I am a good spearman, both on foot and on horseback.' Thus equipped, he ruled most of the Near East for 36 years from 522 BC, extending and consolidating an empire that reached to India and the borders of Greece.

A WOMAN'S PLACE

Women's lives were dominated by the need to provide children – vital for the

survival of the family. Wives were meant to be subject to their husbands, yet Biblical

accounts include plenty of forceful women who take charge of their own destinies.

A LAW TABLET from Ashur, capital of Assyria around the presumed time of Moses in the 13th century BC, states with chilling specificity: 'A gentleman may flog his wife, he may pull out her hair, he may damage and twist her ears. There is nothing wrong in this.'

But, despite such codes, actual marital relations were rarely harsh, and touchingly familiar sentiments light up the dusty tablets of correspondence pulled from ancient sites. Such is the case with a letter to a 13th-century BC queen of Ugarit, on the coast of Canaan opposite Cyprus, from her mother in inland Amurru. 'May the gods of Ugarit and the gods of Amurru keep you in the best of health', the mother politely began. Then, getting to the heart of the matter: 'Are things going well between you and the king? I want an answer.'

Mesopotamian women in the 2nd millennium BC had rights under law, could engage in business, own property and testify in court. They were employed in

WATCHING An ivory carving shows a woman – possibly a prostitute – at a window.

cloth manufacture (though paid less than men), and brewing was a thriving cottage industry largely run by women, who were also innkeepers and pawnbrokers. Professional opportunities were greatest in religious life, where high priestesses reigned over certain temples.

Divorce was an equitable arrangement with special provisions for abandoned wives. Under Babylonian laws of 1700 BC, a man divorcing a wife because she was barren had to pay her a bounty. A wife who had neglected her household duties to pursue outside interests could be let go with nothing. But if she could not endure her husband and was of good character she departed with her 'bride price' – a betrothal nest egg deposited by the groom's family as a form of insurance.

Under another Mesopotamian law, a husband could not favour one wife over another in his will, and even a concubine was provided for if she bore him children – as long as the man's wife remained

---

EYEWITNESS

A MOTHER'S LULLABY TO HER SON

FOUR THOUSAND YEARS AGO in the Mesopotamian city of Ur a royal mother coaxed to sleep her infant son with this lullaby, the first one that we know of:

❛ *Ooh-ah . . . Ah-ooh-a . . .*
  As I coo, may my baby grow,
  As I coo, may he grow strong,

Firmly rooted as the irina tree,
Noble as the shakir plant.
Down among the apple trees by
  the river,
Sleep will spread over him.
Sleep, my son, sleep is overtaking
  you.
Sleep is settling over you.

Come Sleep, come Sleep,
Come to where my son lies,
Hurry, Sleep, to where my son lies.
Put to sleep his restless eyes,
Put your hand on his painted eyes
  and his babbling tongue –
Let not the babbling hold back
  his sleep. ❜

INTO WEDLOCK **The fathers of a bride and groom agree a marriage contract which a scribe writes down.**

childless the concubine's children were his heirs. Even so, marriage was a firmly one-sided affair. Whereas a husband could take a second wife and cohabit with as many concubines or slave girls as he had the price and desire for, extramarital sex was strictly forbidden to a wife.

Sex laws were designed to promote family stability. A Hittite might have sex with his step-mother once she was widowed, but this was a 'criminal abomination' should his father be still alive; adultery with a sister-in-law or mother-in-law were likewise capital offences.

For the Israelites, the Book of Numbers laid down an elaborate procedure if a man suspected his wife of infidelity. He was to bring her before a priest who would 'take holy water in an earthen vessel, and take some of the dust that is on the floor of the tabernacle and put it into the water'. After various rituals, the priest made the woman drink the water. Then: 'If she has defiled herself and has acted unfaithfully against her husband, the water that brings the curse shall enter into her and cause bitter pain, and her body shall swell, and her thigh shall fall away [that is, she would lose the ability to bear children], and the woman shall become an execration among her people. But if the woman has not defiled herself and is clean, then she shall be free and shall conceive children.'

The extent to which penalties were applied in such cases is debatable; wronged husbands did not have to press charges and in many societies a woman accused of infidelity could clear herself by swearing her innocence before a god. Causing public scandal seems to have been the real sin. Gossipmongering was discouraged: a man who slandered someone else's wife could be arrested and given a distinctive haircut as an object lesson.

EQUALITY AND SUBJUGATION

Relations between the sexes were more relaxed among the Egyptians, who delighted in family companionship and romantic love. Few men of means were monogamous, but the senior wife was her husband's partner, her status secure and the household goods hers under law; widows ran the family business if there was no son old enough to take over. Contraception and abortion were both illegal in Egypt, but the situation was as ambiguous as it has been in most cultures, since prescriptions for both were available.

The Assyrians were quite different. Under their law from the 12th century BC, a wife became her husband's chattel. Mutilations were meted out to their women for assorted misdemeanours. At their husbands' pleasure, their eyes might be gouged out, or a nose lopped off. For harbouring a runaway wife without her husband's knowledge, an Assyrian woman could lose her ears. A law

FAMILY GODDESS **Many Canaanite households had figurines of the fertility goddess Astarte – also worshipped at times by the Israelites.**

CELEBRATION: AN ISRAELITE WEDDING

A MARRIAGE was binding from the moment of betrothal, even though it might be some time before the couple actually started living together. The wedding was not a ceremony, but a prolonged celebration commencing when the groom claimed his bride and brought her home.

First came the processions. The groom set out, dressed in his best clothes and garlanded with flowers, accompanied by a retinue of cheering and bantering friends. Waiting at her father's house was the bride, veiled and bedecked in all the finery she could muster, topped by the jewellery that was the customary marriage gift from her husband.

The procession then retraced its steps, larger now and gathering further strength and boisterous hilarity along the way as neighbours and the merely curious joined the cheerful parade.

The father of the groom declared open house – a 'house of feasting' – for as long as his food, wine and funds held out: it could be for a week, or even longer. The climax was the marriage feast. As well as eating and drinking to excess, there were music, songs, dances, jokes and games, and an exchange of gifts. The prophet Jeremiah, ably abetted by the Biblical translators of Shakespearean England, captures the spirit perfectly: 'The voice of mirth and the voice of gladness, the voice of the bridegroom and the voice of the bride.'

When it was over, the new wife faced a traumatic readjustment. If she was well-to-do, she would have brought her own maid – her slave – with her; perhaps more than one. Otherwise, she suddenly found herself totally alone, her fate in the hands of a husband she hardly knew and a mother-in-law who would rule as mistress of the extended household for as long as her husband's father still lived.

against abortion was uniquely brutal: 'They shall impale her on stakes without burying her.' Where the culprit had died as a result of the abortion, the punishment was exacted on her body.

Under the Assyrians, a head covering – not necessarily a full veil – became an instrument of both status and subjugation. Upper-class wives were forbidden to go out with their heads uncovered, while concubines and prostitutes, by contrast, were actually prohibited from covering their heads under pain of a flogging. Veiling a concubine before witnesses was a formal act by which a man acknowledged her as a wife.

RULES FOR WOMEN

The female biological cycle and concerns for ritual purity resulted in many regulations; these are some:
Mesopotamian textile workers were given leave with pay during their menstrual periods.
The period of an Israelite mother's 'uncleanness' after giving birth to a daughter was twice that after giving birth to a son.
In Judah, sexual intercourse during menstruation was a crime punishable by banishment in the 6th century BC.

Divorce for men was made supremely simple and painless: 'If a gentleman wishes to divorce his wife, if it is his will, he may give her something. If it is not his will, he need not give her anything; she shall go out empty.'

THE EROTIC TRAP

Israelite attitudes reflected this cultural buffeting from different neighbouring peoples. The sensuality of the Old Testament was basic and earthy. 'Let her breasts satisfy thee at all times; and be thou ravished always with her love', Proverbs counsels, while the Song of Solomon is a peerless paean to erotic pleasure ('he shall lie all night betwixt my breasts . . . '). Yet the alluring woman capable of turning a man's head could also be a threat to family stability, a constant danger. Proverbs warns against the bored wife whose husband is away on business and who 'with harlot's attire and subtle heart' leads the unwary male 'like an ox to the slaughter'.

Legally, the Israelite woman's husband was her 'baal', a word equally applied to livestock ownership, just as Baal – in the sense of 'Lord' – was how the Canaanites addressed their most powerful god. Her husband could throw her out at any time; he could also humiliate her by acquiring and favouring a younger wife. Divorce was a private matter in which she had no legal say.

VILLAGE WEDDING Friends feast and dance while the bride and groom sit and watch from the shade of a fig tree.

A Son's Praise of His Mother

THIS ODE written in Nippur, 100 miles (160 km) north of Ur, sings the praises of a mother, also cataloguing the things most admired in ancient Mesopotamia.

❛ Her name is Shatishtar . . . radiant of figure.
A lovely goddess, a daughter-in-law of delight
Blessed from her girlhood, energetic in managing the house of her father-in-law, . . .
Vigilant, she multiplied possessions;
Beloved, cherished, full of life,
Lamb, cream, honey, flowing butter of my heart.

My mother is the bright light of the horizon, a mountain deer, the morning star,
Precious carnelian, topaz, jewel of a princess, full of allure;
A ring of tin, bracelet of iron, staff of gold and bright silver;
A charming ivory figurine, an angel in alabaster upon a lapis lazuli pedestal.

My mother is the rain in season, water for the seeds,
A rich harvest, finest barley, a garden of plenty,
Fruit of the New Year, a New Year offering,

A canal bearing enriched water to the irrigation ditches,
The sweetest Dilmun date, most desired of all dates.
A feast, an offering of rejoicing, a chant of abundance, a dancing place of joy.

My mother is a pine chariot, a litter of boxwood,
A fine garment perfumed with oil,
An ostrich shell filled with prime oil,
A glorious garland.
Ludingirra, your beloved son, greets you! ❜

LOOKING GLASS   Mirrors like this Canaanite one from the 14th century BC were made of polished bronze.

Salvation for the Israelite woman lay above all in her usefulness in the home and in the sons she bore. A son grew up deeply respecting his mother and when he brought home a wife, the mother ruled her daughter-in-law as her husband ruled her. A girl became a wife as swiftly as nature and her marketability made it possible, and her immediate object was to bear sons.

TRAUMA OF CHILDBIRTH

'Give me children or I die', Rachel cries to her husband in Genesis. Both are to be her fate. Death in childbirth was a harsh aspect of life in all societies until modern times. Based upon the evidence of recovered remains, the average life span of an Israelite woman was hardly 30 years whereas men, spared the dangers of reproduction, lived an average ten years longer.

Childbirth was traumatic, especially so in the isolated circumstances of village life, where a woman would have only female family members to help her. Experienced midwives were available in towns, but the Israelites took stubborn pride in a self-sufficient hardiness. 'The Hebrew women are not as the Egyptian women; for they are lively and are delivered before the midwives come in unto them,' boasts Exodus. There was recourse to charms and hocus-pocus potions.

For all the perils of childbearing, failure to conceive was worse. If a wife remained barren, she could resort to the use of magic or aphrodisiacs to try to correct the situation – mandrake roots are cited in the Bible.

If a man died before fathering a son, his brother or closest male relative was obliged to marry or at very least impregnate the widow in order to perpetuate the dead man's name by fathering a legal heir. The Genesis story of Tamar is particularly instructive of the various social pressures. Twice-widowed and still without children, Tamar disguises herself as a prostitute in order to seduce her father-in-law, who has balked at giving her his third and only remaining son. Tamar becomes pregnant as a result of the encounter. Her father-in-law wants her burnt for prostitution, but she is cleared when she reveals the circumstances. She crowns her triumph by giving birth to twin boys.

The moral of the tale was clear to any Israelite: a man reneged on his duty to a childless widow at his peril. Tamar's behaviour was not at issue. Patronising prostitutes carried little or no stigma. Women were free to give or sell themselves – so long as they were not married.

THE IDEAL WIFE

Israelite housewives were domestic managers who had to acquire a range of skills. The idealised 'virtuous wife' of the Book of Proverbs whose 'price is far above rubies' bears responsibility for the family's economic as well as physical well-being. Up before dawn to attend to breakfast, she is adept enough in

MOTHER TO BE A pregnant woman clutches her belly in a 7th-6th century BC figurine. Less than half of all babies reached maturity – hence the pressure on women to bear as many children as possible.

business to make an astute land purchase, which by her own efforts she turns into a vineyard.

Through her spinning and weaving she keeps the family in winter cloaks. By making and selling linen garments she is able to afford for herself silk robes shot through with finest Phoenician dyes, and also to donate to the poor. She is devout and a social asset: 'She openeth her mouth with wisdom, and her tongue is the law of kindness.' The principal beneficiary of all this is her husband, who leaves her to manage everything as he whiles away his time with the city elders, nodding complacently whenever they compliment him on his good fortune.

With her child-rearing and social responsibilities set aside, it would still have taken the typical village wife more than ten hours of nonstop activity to get through her daily routine of household and other tasks. There never could have been enough children . . . to collect fuel for the fire, to help with the water-carrying, baking, washing, spinning and garment-making, and dozens of lesser chores such as charging and tending the oil lamps.

The Old Testament contains a total of 1425 names, of which only 111 are those of women – a telling reflection of the extent of male dominance in public affairs, since these are the focus of the Biblical narrative. Yet no sense of submissiveness or passivity is conveyed.

Biblical women show initiative when the opportunity arises and their bravery is never in doubt. One of the earliest Biblical passages is the Song of Deborah, which tells how Jael the Kenite woman lures and

WOMEN'S WORK Israelite village women, helped by their daughters, spin, weave, grind corn and bake bread.

kills the enemy general Sisera by hammering a tent peg into his skull. The barbaric yet beautiful Song concludes with a description of Sisera's wife, peering from her window, anxiously awaiting his return.

The Israelite priesthood was exclusively male, but kings consulted prophetesses as well as prophets. There were also sorceresses credited with conjuring up the dead – a risky business that could incur the death penalty.

ROYAL WOMEN

Royal harems were state assets passed down with the crown. As in the celebrated case of Solomon's legendary tally of 700 wives and 300 concubines, members of the harem often included foreign princesses acquired as tribute or in diplomatic exchanges – living peace treaties. Their fate was lifelong pampered boredom, unless abruptly plucked away as some conqueror's booty.

The Egyptian monarchy was exceptional. The throne of the pharaohs descended in the female line and, as a consequence of this unique arrangement, queens and princesses played dynamic roles in Egyptian politics. Arabian queens doubled as high priestesses and consequently also wielded power in their own right. Persian kings, while not skimping on concubines, had few wives, and several had only

one, magnifying her standing. Persian royal women were strong-willed, immensely rich from their own private estates and able to exert real influence, sometimes to bloodthirsty effect.

Mothers of kings enjoyed special status and exerted influence upon and through their sons. Very occasionally, an exceptional one achieved real power. For five years from 810 BC the Assyrian Empire was ruled by a woman, Sammuramat, until her son Adad-nirari III reached maturity. It was said that 'nature gave her the body of a woman, yet her deeds made her the equal of the bravest of men'. Her regency was so memorable that she became the subject of legend and inspired the Greek myth of Semiramis, a semidivine being who conquers the world, builds mighty monuments (including Babylon itself) and then changes into a dove.

Israelite tradition enshrined few such fond memories. The rule of women was used by the prophet Jeremiah as a metaphor for disorder, exemplified in Bible history by the wicked doings of Jezebel in the turbulent 9th century BC.

Jezebel was a Phoenician princess whose marriage to King Ahab in about 874 BC sealed an alliance between Israel and Tyre. She dominated her husband like no other Israelite queen and was consigned to history as a symbol of pernicious femininity. One of the worst stories recorded against her concerned a man called Naboth who had a vineyard close to Ahab's palace that the king wanted to acquire and to turn into a vegetable garden. Naboth, however, refused to sell and as a result Ahab went into a deep sulk, refusing to eat. Jezebel took more positive action. She had two ne'er-do-wells accuse Naboth – falsely – of cursing God and the king. Hearing this charge of blasphemy, the elders and nobles of Naboth's city, also acting on Jezebel's orders, stoned him to death . . . allowing Ahab to take possession of the vineyard.

Details of Jezebel's gruesome fate in 842 BC, seen as a punishment for such outrages, are savoured by the Biblical writer. She was flung from a window on the orders of King Jehu, a former general who had overthrown Ahab and Jezebel's son Jehoram. Her body was trampled to pieces by horses and her remains eaten by dogs.

FATEFUL INFLUENCE

Few royal women had a more lasting influence than the comparatively obscure Addaguppi, grandmother of the Biblical Belshazzar. She had already lived through four reigns, including the 43 year span of King Nebuchadnezzar, the destroyer of Jerusalem, when she saw her son Nabonidus, a distinguished general, gain the throne of Babylon. Nabonidus revered his mother, and she in turn revered the sun-god Sin; as king, he strove to impose worship of Sin as the state religion.

Addaguppi died in 547 BC 'happy in that piety which Sin, king of all gods, has planted in my heart'. She was 104 years old. We have her final thoughts: 'My eyesight was good, my hearing was excellent, my hands and feet were sound, my words well chosen, food and drink agreed with me, my health was fine and my mind happy. I saw my great-great-grandchildren up to the fourth generation in good health and had my fill of a fine old age.'

Addaguppi's hold over her son changed the course of history. Nabonidus's religious reforms so outraged the Babylonian establishment that, within a few years, the conqueror Cyrus the Great of Persia was welcomed as a virtual liberator, which is what he was to become for the Judaeans – previously taken captive by the Babylonians – and for their religion.

As a postscript, Cyrus lost his life to an equally strong-willed woman of a very different kind. Campaigning in 530 BC against nomadic marauders near the Caspian Sea, he was killed in battle against a Scythian tribe whose Queen Tomyris led the attack. The skull of Cyrus became the warrior queen's prize drinking cup.

FACE OF POWER The death mask of a queen of the 18th dynasty reflects the high status of royal women in Egypt.

SPINNING FOR ALL
Even high-born women did their share of tasks such as spinning. This Elamite lady of the 8th or 7th century BC is being fanned by a slave as she works.

THE LIFE OF A SLAVE

Slavery was an accepted part of life in Old Testament times. Prisoners of war were often enslaved;

those in financial trouble could sell themselves, and their families, into slavery. In some

Near Eastern societies, slaves owned property and rose to high positions in royal service.

ANY WELL-TO-DO HOUSEHOLD had its slave, or slaves; even the most respectable family was liable to have a slave relative, such were the vicissitudes of Old Testament life.

Slavery was at least as old as the Sumerians in the early 3rd millennium BC, who conducted pre-emptive strikes against the envious tribes beyond their fertile plain and came to realise that it was wasteful to slaughter enemies who could be put to work. Their word for slave was 'mountain man' or 'mountain woman'; the name in their pictograph form of writing is rendered as a combination of the outline of a person of either gender and a mountain.

From long before the time of Abraham, the kings of Ur and other city-states organised their captives in camps and had them digging canals, tilling crown lands and constructing fortifications. Others, 'dedicated' to various deities, were put to work on temple estates. Yet mass slavery of a kind known in Roman times never developed, largely because an adequate supply of labour was available for hire at rates low enough to outperform gangs of unmotivated slaves. Around 1275 BC the Assyrian king Shalmaneser I, put out the eyes of 14 000 captives with the idea of making them more tractable, but this experiment proved counter-productive and was not repeated.

SLAVES WHO SOLD THEMSELVES

Instead, new kinds of servitude developed with the growth of commerce and the accompanying divisions of wealth and poverty. Landless peasants sold themselves for a guaranteed meal and a place to sleep. Parents sold children, and a man in desperate straits might temporarily trade in his entire family, himself included, in order to pay off his debts.

FOR THE LOVE OF A CONCUBINE

AS A SYMBOL of a man's love for a woman, the Hanging Gardens of Babylon are rivalled only by the Taj Mahal of 17th-century AD India.

As classic Greek writers describe them, the gardens rose in terraces, garlanded with flowers and trees and fed by water raised from the Euphrates. They were said to have been built by King Nebuchadnezzar II for his favourite concubine, Amytis, because she pined for the beautiful mountain meadows of her Median homeland lying to the south of the Caspian Sea. They were so stunning that they were ranked second to the pyramids of Egypt among the seven wonders of the ancient world.

There are no contemporary descriptions, however, and the Greek historian Herodotus does not mention the Hanging Gardens in his description of the city, which he visited in the 5th century BC, a century after Nebuchadnezzar's day. Later classical authors differed in their details. The terraces were said to rise to a height of 75 ft (23 m), but one report made the structure much bigger. Some descriptions suggested a Greek misinterpretation of a Mesopotamian ziggurat (a temple structure, shaped like a terraced pyramid) or a confusion between a Persian garden and their own terraced hillsides.

Archaeologists excavating near Nebuchadnezzar's palace came upon vaulted foundations which might have held up the Gardens, but this has been strongly disputed. Envisioning them has challenged artists down the ages.

CAPTIVE, BOUND
A prisoner of war has his arms tied behind his back in an Egyptian statuette. Such captives were usually set to work as slaves.

Self-enslavement was not always an option of desperation. Individuals with more ambition than wealth had the right to raise capital by pledging themselves or a family member as security for a loan. The loan might be worked off, starting immediately, through an agreed period of servitude, but usually the terms called for the borrower's enslavement only in the event of default. With interest rates commonly at 20 per cent and upwards, that could easily happen.

Privately owned slaves were liable to be flogged for attempting to escape and branded, sometimes with the warning: 'Runaway. Seize me!' On the other hand, they might also engage in business on their own behalf – sometimes with their master supplying the working capital. In that way, they could buy their freedom; twice the purchase price was the redemption rate in Babylonia. A slave could also marry a free spouse, in which case their children were classed as free.

By the 1st millennium BC, Assyrian slaves were dealing in property on their own behalf while running a large portion of the empire's business on behalf of their masters. By the 7th century BC, Babylonian slaves could not only own property, but were able to keep their private assets when sold to a new master and to bequeath their property upon their death.

EVOLUTION OF ISRAELITE SLAVERY

Slaves were at all times an important article of international trade in the ancient Near East. In the 14th century BC, Pharaoh Akhenaton was importing from Canaan consignments of 'fine concubines with no blemish'. The terms of an order he placed with the prince of Gezer, in the coastal hills rising between Jaffa and Jerusalem, were crisply stated: 'Total, 40 concubines at 40 shekels each' with payment in 'gold and silver, turquoise, assorted precious stones, ebony chairs'.

The Israelites fully embraced this slave culture. The Bible relates how a host of Midianites were slain to the last man by a force commanded by Moses. All the married women were also slain, leaving their daughters to be shared out among the victors. This might have made sense to a mobile force on the warpath, but once settled the Israelites spared at least a percentage of their captives and put them to work.

As state slaves, the Israelites' prisoners of war were used in royal-owned industries, such as certain mining projects. The second and larger slave class was privately owned and its members predominantly Israelites like their owners. They included people forced into debt by bad harvests, often victims of exorbitant interest rates on borrowed assets. A creditor was allowed by law to seize and sell such persons.

FOR LIFE Among the Israelites, a slave prepared to stay for life with a family had his ear pierced with an awl.

IITI – A SLAVE OF THE GOLDSMITH OF BABYLON

IITI woke with a start in the home of her new master, the Babylon goldsmith Bel-ibni. It was still dark, but the household was astir and Bel-ibni's voice was raised. He had a commission to fashion adornments for a new statue of the god Marduk and delivery was due.

Iiti was a tomboy with some of the audacity of her mother, who had fled unwelcome betrothal to an overbearing Assyrian soldier-farmer and eventually found sanctuary in servitude. Now her mother was dead and Iiti was 13.

She had learned from kitchen gossip that her master thought she might make a pleasing concubine for his second son, Amel, who was 14 and just beginning to show interest in such matters. She caught her breath at the thought. She was trying to conceal an asthmatic condition, hoping that it would not cause Bel-ibni to exercise the return clause in her purchase contract.

Iiti spent the morning sweeping the courtyard, preparing vegetables and being scolded by her mistress and the steward. Bel-ibni returned from the goldsmiths' bazaar around noon and after a light lunch, he and his wife retired for the siesta.

The meal at dusk was rushed because there was a festival at the local temple that Bel-ibni's wife was determined to attend. She flustered Iiti, who dropped a valuable jar of scented oil, and she swept off promising her a beating. With boyish daring, Amel led the girl into the bustling street and trailed his parents to the temple, where they watched from the shadows cast by torches as a bull was slaughtered.

The pair slipped back unnoticed and Iiti lit the lamps. Once home, Bel-ibni's wife issued instructions for the next day. Iiti was relieved to find that the promised punishment had been forgotten.

Tired to the point of exhaustion, she was soon asleep in her little alcove behind the pantry.

An Israelite slave was an item of property. This is demonstrated in laws pertaining to ox goring, as common then as serious traffic accidents are today. If a slave was fatally gored, the owner of the ox was obliged to pay the owner of the dead slave 30 shekels compensation, but if the ox happened to have killed a free man, then the beast's owner could face capital punishment.

Among the Israelites, a slave could be beaten. If the beating was so severe that the slave died immediately after it, then the master was liable for punishment. But if the slave lingered on for a day or two after the beating, the master was given the benefit of the doubt and exonerated since, as the Book of Exodus succinctly puts it, 'he is his money' – it was, after all, the master's own loss.

Despite this, the life of a domestic slave was not always miserable, or even degrading. It largely depended upon the attitude of the owner. Assured of food and shelter and treated as part of the family by a considerate owner, some slaves must have counted themselves fortunate. The relationship could be close and mutually supportive. A slave's advice

FORCED LABOUR Gangs of slaves heave wood in an 8th-century BC Assyrian relief. Large-scale state projects depended on slave labour.

AT NIGHTFALL In the shade of a melon vine, slaves in a rich home light torches and fill oil lamps from a pitcher.

might be taken, or he might even be made an heir in the case of a childless master. The Biblical Joseph is an example of an Israelite slave rising to positions of high responsibility in the service of the Egyptians.

THE OPTION OF FREEDOM

Happily married life was possible while in bondage, some men taking their families with them into slavery, others marrying fellow slaves. By the 7th century BC the domestic slave of an Israelite

BONDAGE FORETOLD

Bible stories of Israelite bondage in Egypt have striking parallels in the earlier legends of other Near Eastern folk. Anticipating Moses in the bulrushes by 1000 years, the Mesopotamian empire-builder Sargon the Great was said to have been cast adrift in a basket as an infant.

master was given an option of release after six years. If he had a wife from his previous life, then she and their children went free too, but if his owner had provided him with a slave wife, then she and any children they might have were taken from him, since these remained the master's property.

The master was supposed to give his departing slave provisions to set himself up as a free man. 'Supply him liberally from your flock, your threshing floor and your winepress', enjoins the Book of Deuteronomy. 'Give to him as the Lord your God has blessed you.' Moreover, the master was told not to be grudging about it all: 'Do not consider it a hardship to set your servant free, because his service to you these six years has been worth twice as much as that of a hired hand.'

In spite of such admonitions, some owners were clearly reluctant to let their slaves go and the six-year rule was widely ignored. The last king of Judah, Zedekiah, in the 6th century BC, tried to put

ALL ROPED UP **An Egyptian wall painting shows bound Syrian prisoners being dragged along by their ropes.**

this right, instituting a covenant with the people of Jerusalem whereby they agreed to set their Hebrew slaves free. They did so but then, according to the Biblical account, changed their minds and forced the newly emancipated slaves back into bondage. This incensed the prophet Jeremiah, speaking in the name of Yahweh:

'I [Yahweh] said, "Every seventh year each of you must free any fellow Hebrew who has sold himself to you. After he has served you for six years, you must let him go free." Your fathers, however, did not listen to me or pay attention to me. Recently you repented and did what is right in my sight. Each of you proclaimed freedom to his countrymen. You even made a covenant before me in the house that bears my Name. But now you have turned round and profaned my name; each of you has taken back the male and female slaves you had set free to go where they wished.'

A Hebrew slave could voluntarily forgo the chance of liberty. He had to make the formal declaration: 'I love my master, my wife, and my children. I will not go out free.' Then he had his ear pierced at the front door as a mark of his commitment to

lifetime servitude. Such 'permanent' slaves were at least in theory subject to release once every 50 years – a measure designed to prevent the creation of a slave caste. Other societies had similar regulations, some more generous.

Outright slavery was not the only form of enforced servitude. Kings frequently resorted to a system perfected in Egypt. The pyramids and other great monuments were not built by slaves, but by a public impressment: an obligatory call-up, which in the case of Egyptians was a religious duty stemming from a tradition of service to the god-pharaoh.

King Solomon in 960 BC had a supply of state slaves, captives from local wars, but not enough for the public works he had in mind, in particular a temple and palace for himself in Jerusalem. According to the Biblical statistics, Solomon raised a levee of some 30 000 men to cut down cedars in the mountains of Phoenicia, and another 150 000 to hew and haul stones. If remotely accurate, it means that every able-bodied subject must have been impressed. Presumably Solomon followed the Egyptian practice of a staggered call-up. In the event, 'Solomon's glory' caused social unrest and economic dislocation.

CLOTHES, FASHIONS, FURNISHINGS

A tunic known as the *kuttoneth* was the basic garment of the Israelites, adorned for

important people with tassels, hems and girdles. Home furnishings were sparse,

except among the very wealthy who enjoyed such luxuries as ivory-inlaid beds.

IN AN AGE when most people had few possessions, a garment was precious and a quality cloak especially so: it was a favourite gift of Persian kings. At the Amorite court of Mari in the 2nd millennium BC, distinguished guests each wore a special robe provided by their royal host, and there was much heart-burning among those courtiers denied this honour. A prize of garments was fitting for a royal wager in Solomon's time and a 'goodly Babylonian mantle' was as much temptation as a hoard of gold and silver in the story of Achan, who committed the capital offence of filching from Joshua's war plunder.

Clothes were handed down, and were a poor person's bank, since they could be given in pledge. This custom became so abused that Israelite law-makers slapped an injunction on a creditor holding a poor man's cloak overnight, for, as they pointed out, 'what else is he going to sleep in?'

FROM SHEEP'S BACKS TO PEOPLE'S BACKS

For the peasant majority, making one's own clothes meant what it said, from sheep's back or flax patch onwards. Wool had to be washed and carded, spun and woven. The spinning wheel would not be invented for another 2000 years, and spinning was done with a simple hand spindle requiring great dexterity. It was usually a woman's task. Weaving was also tedious work, sometimes done by men. 'My days are swifter than a weaver's shuttle, and are spent without hope,' the Biblical Job mulls disconsolately.

ANCIENT T-SHIRT **Tunics like this one found in Egypt were for centuries a common garment in the Near East.**

The Egyptians led in both weaving and spinning, and it has been calculated that 1 lb (450 g) of their finest thread would have stretched a good 60 miles (100 km). Fine linen imported from Egypt was for the rich. Cotton was not introduced to the Near East from India until 700 BC and was a luxury even then. Silk was virtually unheard of, though there is evidence that a little might have begun to trickle along the trade routes from the Far East.

We have only one contemporary illustration of a band of rovers from the time of Abraham. Most are wearing a loose, brightly patterned garment hitched over one shoulder. Some of the men go bare-chested, with a skirt or kilt. All the men are neatly bearded; the women have headbands and shoulder-length hair. The men wear sandals, the women comfortable-looking boots. From their bows, spears and axes and the portable bellows on the back of one of their donkeys they recall the Biblical Kenites, itinerant desert smiths.

The kilt endured as practical military attire, but the basic everyday garment at most times was the *kuttoneth*, a kind of stretched T-shirt reaching to the knees,

LASTING DESIGN
Sandals had a thong passing between the big and second toes and around the ankle.

sometimes to the ankles. A sash belt held weapons and created a pocket for valuables stuffed down the shirt top. To 'gird up thy loins' was to hitch up the garment under the belt, prior to work for which it might get in the way or which might result in it getting soiled. In chilly weather both sexes wore a cloak or mantle, which could be held out to carry a load, and which also did duty as a blanket at night.

A pair of shoes was so taken for granted that it was used as an expression meaning insignificant, like 'two pins' or 'tuppence'. It was an Israelite custom for a property sale to be sealed by the seller taking off a shoe and giving it to the purchaser; in certain circumstances a man judged remiss in meeting his social responsibilities might have his shoes forcibly removed as a form of social stigmatisation.

Under 7th-century BC Israelite law, a childless widow spurned by a brother-in-law (duty-bound to marry her in order to carry on his late brother's line of descent) was empowered to confront the man and in the presence of the elders to 'loose his shoe from off his foot, and spit in his face'. The Hittites had a similar tradition. A soldier caught shirking guard duty was disciplined by the humiliation of having his shoes removed.

Throughout the Near East, elaborate hems and dangling tassels were symbols of rank. An episode in the Biblical narrative in which David snips off the hem of Saul's garment is significant in that he is symbolically weakening the king's authority. The sculpted record of King Jehu offering tribute to the Assyrians in 842 BC provides the only direct glimpse of Israelite royalty (*see page 49*). In the relief, Jehu wears a

fringed kuttoneth, like a modern Arab *galabiyeh*, tied with a tasselled girdle. His attendants have fringed mantles. Both the king and his men have beards trimmed to a point and are wearing floppy caps and sandals with upturned toes.

Popular taste was for bright colour lacking in subtlety – reds and scarlet predominated. Blue was a costly dye which carried particular prestige. The prophet Ezekiel could not but admire the feared Assyrians 'clothed with blue, captains and commanders, handsome young men riding upon horses'. Even a poor Israelite was expected to wear a few blue threads in the tassels of his garments, in accordance with a divine instruction to 'put upon the fringe of the borders a ribband of blue'.

FASTIDIOUS FASHIONS

Fashion-consciousness started young according to a son's letter to his mother from the time of King Hammurabi of Babylon in the 18th century BC. 'Gentlemen's clothes improve year by year', states the boy whose father Shamash-hazir was a high official in royal service. He then bluntly accuses his mother of failing to keep up with these improvements, indeed of trying to cheat on her son's clothing: 'You are the one making my clothes cheaper year by year. By cheapening and scrimping my clothes you have become rich.' Bitterly he makes the comparison with another boy 'whose father is only an underling of my father'. This boy had received 'two new

ALL WEIGHTED DOWN
A reconstructed loom of the kind used in Old Testament times shows the clay weights that kept the yarn taut.

MARKET DELIGHTS   A bejewelled woman examines the textiles on offer in a market at the gates of an Israelite city.

garments, but you keep getting upset over just one garment for me. Whereas you gave birth to me, his mother acquired him by adoption, but whereas his mother loves him, you do not love me.'

DEATH AND THE TAXMAN

People were paying death duties in 2500 BC. Tax collectors hovered around the graveyard in the Sumerian city of Lagash and exacted dues from bereaved families in the form of bread, beer and furnishings. Divorce was also taxed, until a new king came to the throne and, in history's first recorded fiscal reform, eliminated this tax and slashed death duties by half.

Physical condition, as well as good clothing, was important. Cripples suffered scorn; among the Israelites even baldness could carry something of a stigma, according to a Biblical reference in which children bait the prophet Elisha with the chant of 'Baldie! Baldie!'

A luxuriant crop of hair was considered manly, and so was a beard. For grandeur, nothing could compare with the spade-like Mesopotamian beard, fastidiously curled and brought to full glory by the Assyrians. Among the Israelites, King David's son Absalom was famously handsome and his hair was regarded as particularly fine. According to the Biblical writer, 'in all Israel there was no one so much praised for his beauty as Absalom; from the sole of his foot to the crown of his head there was no

THE ISRAELITES AND THE AGE OF IRON

NOT COINCIDENTALLY, Iron and the Israelites were forged at about the same time, for weapons made of the devastating new metal ripped apart the old political order, allowing new peoples and nations to emerge around 1200 BC.

Gold – alluring and occurring naturally in its pure form – was the first metal worked, but it is too soft to be of much practical use. Silver and lead followed. These were produced together by roasting a shiny ore known as galena over a wood fire. Copper was the first practical metal. It was malleable and capable of being hammered to become reasonably hard.

Pottery kilns generated enough heat to extract pure copper from the greenish ore known as malachite and by the 5th millennium BC copper weapons and tools were in use in the Near East. Bronze is stronger, easier to cast and less subject to corrosion. Production of this copper-tin alloy was perfected by about 2600 BC to give the first empires their cutting edge and expand

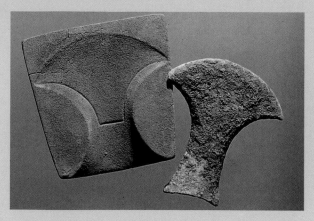

BRONZE AGE This bronze axe head, with the mould used to cast it, dates from the 10th century BC. By then iron was replacing bronze in tools and weapons.

trade networks in an urgent quest for rare tin ores.

Iron had long been known from the content of chance finds of meteorites, but its high melting point required furnace improvements before it could be extracted from natural ores. Ore heated to 1200°C (2200°F) produced a spongy mass, that had to be laboriously hammered while hot. A few soft iron objects were being made in this way by 2000 BC.

The most important advances in metallurgy were made in the north-east of modern Turkey and Armenia, where many ores were locally available. It was here some time after 1500 BC that Hittite smiths mastered a way of hardening wrought iron by repeated reheating with charcoal in a process now known as carburising. Subsequent sudden cooling by quenching in water or oil produces steel. By 1000 BC this, too, was known.

Ironworking was the nuclear technology of the time, its secrets jealously guarded. The Hittite kings exercised a near monopoly on hardened iron for several generations, but the breakup of their empire in the 13th century BC stimulated its spread. Its reverberations are reflected in the 11th-century BC Israelites' discomfort in facing the iron-armed Philistines.

Iron's greatest impact was not on warfare, but on farming, construction and manufacturing. By the 10th century BC, iron ploughs and sickles, chisels and saws were coming into use, their sharper edges revolutionising carpentry, stonemasonry and crop production and stimulating commerce in general.

---

blemish in him'. The writer goes on to describe how the prince cut his hair once a year – when it became 'heavy on him' – and weighed it. It came apparently to '200 shekels by the king's weight', or approximately 5 lb (2.3 kg).

The fundamentalist Rechabites did not cut their hair, nor did the Biblical super-hero Samson. The notion that a warrior drew strength from his hair was a widely held tradition in the Near East. The close-cropped, clean-shaven Egyptians were as different in this as in many other customs.

Keeping hair clean, and cleanliness in general, presented a problem where water was scarce and soap was primitive. Some homes had portable washbasins and the upper class provided footbaths for arriving visitors to wash off the dirt of travel. But people relied more upon oil than water, risking lice rather than fleas.

The ubiquitous olive oil was slapped on the head as well as the body, and augmented with scents to the extent affordable. Garments were sprinkled with myrrh, aloe and other fragrances, and an application of scented oils helped to mask the fug of smelly woollens.

Mirrors were made of polished bronze, but these were a luxury, and putting on make-up must have

JEWEL BOX These necklaces, rings and earrings, along with their box, came from a 13th-century BC Canaanite tomb. A woman's jewellery was an important asset that could be exchanged for other goods.

been a trial for many women. Despite this and the Israelite prophets' distaste for 'painted faces', cosmetics were liberally applied – crushings of red ochre or henna leaves to cheeks, hands, feet or hair, and other clay-plant mixtures. Eyes were lined with a gummy iron or antimony-based substance that also acted as a disinfectant.

A WALKING VAULT

Even a poor woman had beads and bangles, while the rich lady jangled and stumbled under the weight of pendants, chains and necklaces. She was a walking bank vault, for like the poor man's frayed cloak these were her negotiable assets.

The prophet Isaiah, denouncing the vanities of his time and invoking a day of judgment on its women, gave an inventory of their ornaments: 'In that day the Lord will take away the finery of the anklets, the headbands, and the crescents; the pendants, the bracelets, and the scarfs; the headdresses, the armlets, the sashes, the perfume boxes, and the amulets; the signet rings and nose rings; the festal robes, the mantles, the cloaks, and the handbags; the garments of gauze, the linen garments, the turbans, and the veils. Instead of perfume there will be rottenness; and instead of a girdle, a rope; and instead of well-set hair, baldness; and instead of a rich robe, a girding of sackcloth; instead of beauty, shame.'

Men also scented and ornamented themselves, and no woman's cosmetic armoury could compare with the exotic wonders borne in the Persian King Darius II's travelling 'ointment chest'. They included a skin cream made from an opium gum boiled in lion's fat, to which saffron and palm oil had been added.

Indeed, nothing before, or possibly since, then could match the ostentation and the self-indulgence of Persian royalty. It is calculated that it cost the equivalent of £2 million just to outfit a 5th-century

MAKE-UP TRAY Sandstone cosmetic trays like this one from the 9th century BC were common in ancient Israel.

BC Persian monarch. The king's garb consisted of a long gold-embroidered purple robe, full at the sleeves, over striped tunic and crimson pantaloons. He dripped jewels from ears, neck and wrists, and clasped a gold sceptre. The effect was compared favourably with a peacock in full display.

The king wore a tall, flat-topped cap, called the *kidaris*, with a blue and white tassel, or a crenellated crown on state occasions. His throne was sited under a pillared canopy and was so high that he required a stool to mount it. A bevy of attendants fussed around, faces muffled to protect him from their breath, while censers puffed clouds of incense.

Earlier, the Babylonians had supported similar traditions, and few send-offs could have matched that accorded the redoubtable matriarch Addaguppi, Belshazzar's grandmother, in 547 BC. Her body was

HAIRSTYLES AND HEADDRESSES Women often wore their hair in a long plait, sometimes covered with a shawl. Many men wore pointed caps to protect their heads from the sun.

wrapped in 'shining white linen' and entombed with 'splendid gold ornaments set with precious stones' and jars of scented oil. The tomb was concealed to thwart robbers.

Mourning was declared 'from the Upper Sea to the Lower Sea' (the Red Sea to the Arabian Gulf), and every subject king, prince and governor from around the empire summoned to Babylon, where 'for seven days and seven nights they walked about, heads hung low, ash-strewn, stripped of their attire'.

Nobody was allowed to shave or wash for a week. Then there was a general clean-up, mourning

FURNISHINGS FOR THE DEAD

DEATH THE GREAT LEVELLER was never so in the land of the pharaohs; there and elsewhere in the ancient Near East the wealthy ensured that they departed life in style. Among the Israelites, notions of being 'collected unto one's fathers' and a concomitant need to maintain family bonds beyond the grave became paramount.

In the first Mesopotamian cities and among the early Canaanites, bodies were deposited beneath the home. Health considerations militated against this continuing for too long, although infants continued to be given domestic burial.

Wealthier Israelites had family tombs hewn from the rock in a convenient location beyond the city walls. A typical vault was a chamber reached by a sloping passage, sometimes with other chambers leading off. A stone slab sealed the entrance.

Bodies were placed on shelves, usually with a few possessions, such as personal seals. Small beverage jugs were placed by the corpse, and an oil lamp left alight in a niche, echoes of a belief that the spirit required light and nourishment for its last journey. Many tombs were used for centuries; to make room for new bodies, old bones were deposited in a charnel pit. Interment was on the day of death. The body was dressed in a mantle suitable for the sobriety of Sheol, the gloomy underworld retreat of Israelite souls.

Failure to be buried was the deepest disgrace that could befall a person. To be picked over by scavenging bird and beast was the kind

RESTING PLACE **The bones of a decomposed body were sometimes kept in a carved ossuary.**

of curse that the avenging prophets savoured, and the law stipulated that even executed criminals had to be interred without delay, lest they 'defile the land'. The nearest village was held responsible for burying strangers found by the wayside.

Mourning, which lasted seven days, was a time for loud lamentation. People tore their clothes, put on coarse goat-hair garments (sackcloth), removed their shoes and smeared themselves with dust and ashes. They shaved their heads and their beards and even slashed themselves to draw blood, though that came to be considered excessive.

Dirges were sung – by bands of professional mourners in the case of all who could afford the expense. Family and friends observed a fast, broken by a feast at which 'the cup of consolation' was passed around and sorrows drowned.

BONE STORER **Storing bones in ossuaries made space in a tomb for more recent bodies.**

FUNERAL GRIEF Mourners watch as the carefully wrapped body of a dead relative is taken into a rock tomb.

clothes were thrown away, and to make everybody 'glad and presentable' once more, chests of new clothes and a copious supply of scented oils were distributed gratis for the long journeys home.

THE LURE OF IVORY

The cultural and material attainments of rival courts were a constant spur to royal circles. Thrones were a focus of competition, though a standard model emerged in the 2nd millennium BC. High-backed and placed at the top of steps, its arms were fashioned into fabulous sphinx-like creatures and it had carved ivory inlays. Solomon's lion-festooned throne was of this type, described in the Book of Chronicles: 'The king also made a great ivory throne, and overlaid it with pure gold. The throne had six steps and a footstool of gold, . . . and on each side of the seat were arm rests and two lions standing beside the arm rests, while 12 lions stood there, one on each end of a step on the six steps.'

Ivory was the preferred material of the truly rich, especially on furniture. An ivory-inlaid bed was particularly coveted (to the disgust of the prophet Amos railing against the nobility of his day 'who lie upon beds of ivory, and stretch themselves upon their couches'). There is even a record of one royal bride arriving armed with three such beds. Delicate ivory carving was a Phoenician speciality. Pieces have been found that were numbered, so that they could be fitted correctly in place when delivered to the client. Among ordinary folk, a small ivory item such as a cosmetic spoon was a prized possession.

For his new palace in Samaria, King Ahab in 869 BC ordered cedar walls inlaid with carved ivory. This was the 'ivory house' mentioned in the Bible, and fragments of it have been found. Designs were influenced by Egypt, but the style was charmingly insouciant. An infant god Horus squatting upon a lotus was plumper than in Egyptian versions, for instance, and lions were quaintly gentle. Surfaces were decorated with mosaic insets of reds, blues and greens and gold leaf.

The Philistines introduced elegant pottery styles from the Aegean, with designs in red and black that were as lively as they were distinctive. The Phoenicians were celebrated for their textiles made into garments dyed in hues from soft pink to deep violet.

Much Israelite pottery was rough and ready, without the finish and subtle design of previous Canaanite workmanship or of the Israelites' neighbours, but it improved. Samarian ware of the 8th and 7th centuries BC had an elegant beauty. By this time, workshops were turning out vessels in standardised sizes.

MOLLUSCS AND THE COLOUR PURPLE

A SECRETION of sea snails was the source of the ancient Near East's most highly prized dye: so prized, indeed, that it became an emblem of power and privilege and gave to its producers the name by which they are known to this day – the Phoenicians, or purple people.

It was not purple as we know it now, but rather ranged from violet-blue to a deep purple-red. It came from the decayed innards of two species of a sea snail known as murex, caught with baited nets off Tyre and other Phoenician ports. Each mollusc contributed only a few drops of dye secretion.

The hard shells were smashed open and the contents salted and allowed to rot for a few days before being tipped into a cauldron. Steam was piped into the seething mess, which was cooked for nine days. Floating flesh and shell fragments were then continuously skimmed off until the solution was ready for testing on wool which had been soaked in lye, an alkaline solution made by 'percolating' wood ashes in water. If the result was satisfactory, the wool was immersed in the stew for several hours. Sometimes honey was added. The dyed wool was dried in the sun, producing such a stench that dye factories were sited downwind of towns. A papyrus from the time of Ramses II refers to 'the stink like rotten fish' that a dyer could never wash off, so that 'the man comes to detest any cloth'.

Wool dyed with 'sea purple' was colour-fast and literally worth its weight in gold; it made fortunes for Phoenician merchants. Sea-purple fabric graced the tabernacle of Yahweh. Persian kings draped themselves in purple, held court under a purple canopy, walked on purple carpets. For one purple gown, a celebrated Egyptian courtesan paid 500 times the price she placed on her services. By Roman times, being 'born to the purple' implied a person of aristocratic birth.

PURPLE TRADER
A Phoenician merchant displays some purple cloth, made using a dye obtained from sea snails.

WORK AND PLAY IN THE BIBLICAL WORLD

The ancient Near East was a place of much coming and going. Great cities like

Babylon were huge cosmopolitan centres bringing together people from all over

the known world. Empires waxed and waned, subjecting one nation to another –

in the relief above Israelite officials pay tribute to the Assyrian king Shalmaneser.

The arts of war became more sophisticated; the arts of leisure – feasting,

music and dance – remained a vital release from the toil of everyday living.

LIFE AT THE CENTRE

Jerusalem fell to Nebuchadnezzar II of Babylon on March 16, 597 BC – 11 years later Babylonian

forces completed its destruction. Large numbers of Judah's nobility and skilled craftsmen

were deported, thus beginning their period of captivity in the world's most glittering capital.

BABYLON was a heart-thumping sight for the straggling mass of political deportees at the end of their 1000 mile (1600 km) forced march from Jerusalem. Approaching from the north along a bank of the Euphrates, they were shooed up a heavily fortified causeway between high walls shimmering with blue glaze. Before them towered the massive Ishtar Gate. Through its bronze doors spread the fabled city of temples and gardens, topped by the Platform of Heaven and Earth, a seven-step 300 ft (90 m) ziggurat – a terraced temple tower – that inspired the legend of the Biblical tower of Babel.

It was 586 BC and Babylon, 'Gate of the Gods', 'Queen of Asia', was at its zenith as the greatest city in the world.

MIGHTY BEAST Lining the Processional Way into Babylon were 120 lions in glazed brick.

PEOPLE-MOVING POLICIES

Mass deportations were a favourite ploy of ancient empire-builders, as common an occurrence as floods of refugees in modern times. They eradicated potential hotbeds of revolt and provided pools of labour to be deployed wherever a conqueror could best make use of them. Into the vacuums created by the deportations, it was usual to move groups from other parts of the empire.

Though traumatic, deportation was not actual enslavement and the practice had a long-term beneficial effect in mixing cultures and spreading ideas. Even the most hardhearted Assyrian ruler encouraged assimilation and in time the transplanted aliens gained all the social rights of the native population. Sargon II of Assyria, in the decade before 700 BC, was proud of acquiring 'people from the four quarters of strange tongues' and he assigned instructors to school them 'in custom and [how] to serve the gods and the king'.

Generally, the aim was to put to maximum use the most talented members of the conquered group: metalworkers and other craftsmen were especially prized, while military units were often recruited into the victor's armies. They were normally deported to the conqueror's city and set to work there. The common people were left behind. As the Biblical account of the fall of Judah puts it: 'The captain of the guard left the poor of the land to be vinedressers and husbandmen.'

The Israelites were subject to repeated deportations. By 721 BC the northern kingdom of Israel had been wiped out and according to the victor's records 27 230 captives had been removed to Assyria, where they disappeared into oblivion as the 'lost tribes'; in fact, they were probably assimilated. Judah remained prosperous during much of this period. Eventually, however, it too fell into decay and suffered more than one defeat and deportation before the capture of Jerusalem in 597 BC, followed by the city's destruction 11 years later. Scholars estimate the number of Judaeans deported to Babylon at not more than 20 000, but these constituted the intellectual and artisan elite. Instead of finding themselves in some backwater, they were moved to a stimulating cosmopolitan metropolis.

HUB OF THE WORLD

The 43 year reign of Nebuchadnezzar saw Babylon reach a peak as a political and commercial centre. Supremely businesslike, its sophisticated bureaucracy encouraged the development of professions *continued on page 83*

continued on page 83

WORLD'S CENTRE The Ishtar Gate was emblazoned with bulls and dragons, symbols of the gods Adad and Marduk. During Nebuchadnezzar's reign Babylon was the hub of the civilised world, with a population approaching 200 000.

IN ROYAL DAVID'S CITY

King David and his successors converted Jerusalem from a modest fortress town into a great capital.

THE JERUSALEM seized by King David around 1000 BC was a tiny fortress town strung along a thin spur in the Judaean hills, defined by a gully on its eastern side and a broader valley to the west. It had been inhabited since prehistoric times. When the Israelites entered Canaan in the 13th century BC it was a stronghold of the Jebusite tribe who remained there until David captured it.

It was watered by a permanent spring gurgling at its base. Less than 500 yd (460 m) from end to end, and averaging 100 yd (90 m) across, it was 30 miles (48 km) from the Mediterranean as the hawk flew, yet a world away in the reality of the times. Centuries before, the rocky scarp had been steepened to deter invaders and crowned by walls. Its natural defences and location near caravan routes compensated for the space restrictions. By capturing it the Israelites completed the unification of their kingdom.

David's son Solomon almost tripled the city's size by expanding northwards to incorporate a hump of higher ground which had been a sacred 'high place' from antiquity. The summit of the hump measured hardly an acre (0.4 ha) but, by building retaining walls and filling the enclosed slopes, the king created a broad platform on which to build his temple. The gap between the temple site and the old city was largely taken by a palace complex of buildings with thick courses of limestone slabs and beams of Lebanon cedar rafted down the coast from Tyre and then hauled overland.

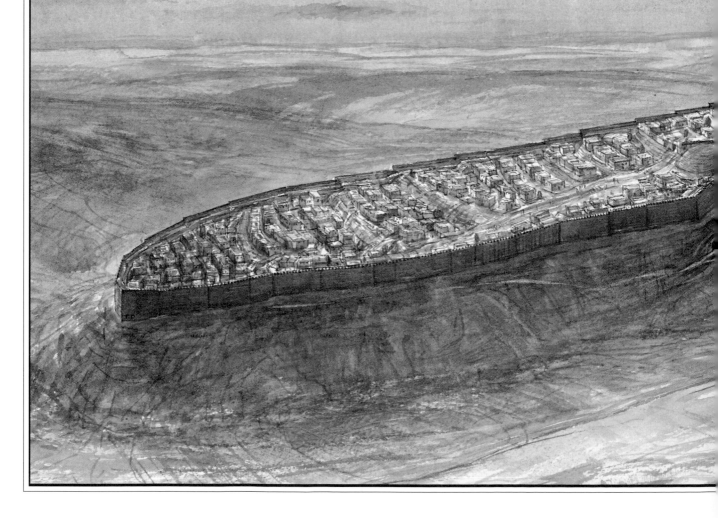

STATELY GIANT The light, resinous wood of the cedar of Lebanon, which grew in huge forests on the mountains above Tyre, made it an ideal building material. Solomon used it in both the Temple and his palace.

Entered from the city, on a rising slope, the first palace structure was the largest. This was a reception hall that according to the Biblical record was 45ft (14m) tall and roofed and pillared with cedar and hung with shields of gold. The Pillared Porch, an anteroom for waiting dignitaries, stood beyond. Then, ascending still, came the sandalwood and cedar-lined Hall of Judgment containing the throne and ivory-inlaid side seating for courtiers. Bronze braziers provided heating in winter. Beyond the throne room and nearest the temple were the royal apartments.

The population of Solomon's city was still small, perhaps 5000, but by Hezekiah's reign late in the 8th century BC the walls enclosed 125 acres (50ha), allowing for a population of about 25 000. Dwellings and bazaars spilling out beyond the walls would eventually bury the western valley under the detritus of centuries of habitation.

SOLOMON'S JERUSALEM The Temple rises from the city's highest point. On the next tier down is the House of the Forest of Lebanon named after its great cedarwood pillars.

PALACE FOR A KING   Monarchs built on a grand scale, enriching their capitals and royal palaces with the fruits of conquest. This relief, showing Chaldean captives, comes from Sennacherib's palace at Nineveh.

Ku-Baba: A Tavern-keeper of Babylon

Ku-Baba rose to the comforting smell of barley malt and the yelp of the guard dog. Her workers were already busily crushing the malted grain and shovelling it into the pit, ready for her to flavour it with a secret recipe of herbs and spices. All of Babylon was restless in anticipation of the approaching New Year festivities. She would need all the beer she could brew or barter, and plenty of wine besides.

Drawn to Ku-Baba's popular establishment off Sin Street was an eclectic crowd of rich and not-so rich officials, merchants and craftsmen, courtesans and bawdy hussies. So, occasionally, were fugitives and other suspicious persons.

Between supervising the preparation of garlands for next week's festival, Ku-Baba spent much of the day balancing her accounts. Dusk saw some of the regulars trickle in, accompanied by a ship's captain up from the Gulf with a performing monkey he hoped to sell. Voices rose, a flute began to trill and an old soldier attempted a dance he half-remembered from somewhere. By

FESTIVE PREPARATIONS Garlands were an essential decoration for festivals.

now the tavern resounded to drinking songs. 'The vat . . . the vat . . . the vat that cheers the liver,' crooned a hoarse baritone.

The tavern emptied gradually and only a handful remained when Hittibel appeared, tired and thirsty from his duties with the Night Watch. Hittibel was a bright young scientist, an official star-watcher and a favourite with Ku-Baba, who enjoyed the enthusiastic way in which he tried to explain to her the mathematical calculations associated with celestial observation.

Laughing, Ku-Baba had to shoo him out. She was as tired as a canal-digger in springtime. Tomorrow would be busier still. She would deliver a judicious offering to her temple-keeper husband's place of worship first thing in the morning.

and specialist crafts, supported by temple treasuries and a banking system employing forms of credit as imaginatively as its modern counterparts.

Babylon's importance sprang from its location on fertile land at the confluence of major trade routes. Its river front bustled with shipping and its temple granaries bulged with the barley and wool. Gangs toiled constantly to clear silt and reeds from irrigation canals that fed its fields and navigation canals linking the Euphrates to the Tigris. Upstream, an artificial reservoir with a 40 mile (64 km) perimeter ensured the city's water supply.

Palm-shaded family plots and orchards lent a rural air to some quarters of the metropolis. Others were loud with the clamour of merchants or the clang of metalworkers. Others again reeked of curing leather, dyeing vats, the charcoal braziers of the goldsmiths or the furnaces of the glass-workers who twirled molten mixtures into exotic and colourful creations. Trades were organised in guilds with father-to-son traditions of apprenticeship.

Holy status and economic clout made temples the gilt-edged financial institutions, but there was also private commercial banking. Merchant bankers financed trade and business ventures. Property, live-stock and slaves could be bought on credit, which could be paid off in instalments. The Babylonians tracked commodity price movements as assiduously as they did river levels and weather statistics.

continued on page 86

83

THE WRITTEN WORD

One of the most important inventions in human history

grew out of the need to keep statistical records.

PICTURE WRITING The Egyptians had established their picture script, known to the Greeks as hieroglyphics ('sacred scratchings'), by 3000 BC.

A BOAST coming from an anonymous scribe in the age of Abraham in the 2nd millennium BC conveys the excitement that accompanied the development and spread of writing: 'Behold! There is nothing better than writing. Being a scribe is the greatest calling of all. There is nothing like it on earth.'

Writing was a Sumerian invention some time before 3200 BC. The earliest specimen known to modern scholars was found at Uruk (Biblical Erech), a community lying a little to the north of Ur on the Euphrates flood plain. Here, the growth of riverside settlements and the emergence of the first city-states made it necessary to keep increasingly complicated records to monitor and manage public works and trade. Some time before 3000 BC people were recording statistical data on pads of river clay that fitted snugly into the palm of the hand. They used a reed point to inscribe notations in the form of sets of symbols. Some were simple abstract forms, others outlines of familiar objects such as a human head.

It was no sudden brainwave. Up to 5000 years earlier, pebble-sized clay tokens in various shapes were in use throughout the Near East as counters to represent livestock

KING AND COMMENTARY A Sumerian tablet shows King Ur-Nanshe of Lagash and his cupbearer with a commentary in cuneiform script.

and other common commodities. The first writing developed as a two-dimensional simplification of this. By 2800 BC considerable advances had been made, with verbs being formed by associating a sign with an action that it brought to mind. Alternatively, two or more different signs were linked, such as the signs for 'mouth' and 'water' to create the verb 'to drink'.

It was also found that a particular species of reed with a triangular cross-section created an effective sharp impression. The wedge-shaped patterns that resulted are called cuneiform (from the Latin *cuneus*, wedge) by archaeologists.

In the Nile basin writing began in a similar way with hieroglyphics established by 3000 BC. The Egyptians also invented pen-and-ink writing, made possible by the manufacture of a kind of paper from papyrus, a local water plant.

By 1800 BC, the scribe was a pivotal figure in Near Eastern societies, essential in the organisation of everything from a military campaign to the running of a temple. Would-be scribes were largely recruited from the upper classes and the vast majority were male, although women were not barred from taking up the profession.

Scribes were intoxicated by their powers and delighted in preparing lists and data on subjects as diverse as glass-making and botany. Numbers were easy to represent as so many strokes, and once special signs were assigned to multiple sets of strokes mathematics, too, progressed using counting systems based on units of 60 and 10. The notion of nothing – zero – presented

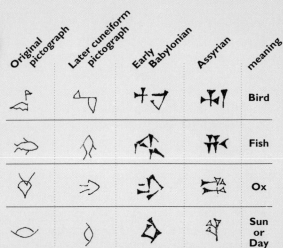

LETTERS TO PHARAOH These tablet letters were dictated by the Canaanite Rib-Addi, Prince of Byblos, around 1370 BC.

Original pictograph	Later cuneiform pictograph	Early Babylonian	Assyrian	meaning
				Bird
				Fish
				Ox
				Sun or Day

SIGN INTO SCRIPT The first pictographs clearly resembled the objects they signified. Later scribes found it easier to streamline these signs into a 'shorthand' of straight lines and curves.

a problem for centuries, sometimes solved by leaving blank spaces, until some time after 700 BC when the Babylonians cracked this one by simply allotting it a sign.

Writing remained, however, a cumbersome art with hundreds of characters that demanded years of specialist training to master. The breakthrough, when it came, emerged from a group of relatively upstart peoples: the Canaanites and associated folk who spoke a Semitic language that made sense when written as a series of consonants. The outcome was the alphabet. Up and down the eastern Mediterranean, from the mountains of Lebanon to the desert of Sinai, people were experimenting with this novel way of writing by 1500 BC.

The idea was brilliantly simple: allot a symbol to each spoken sound. The first attempts at sound-symbols were derived from the old pictographs. 'Head', for instance, was 'rosh' in the Semitic tongue, so the outline of a head became the letter 'r'. By 1300 BC people of the Canaanite port-state of Ugarit were using an alphabetic script of 27 cuneiform characters which allow scholars today to translate their correspondence. By 1000 BC the Phoenicians had perfected the system with a streamlined script that was easier to learn and use.

The Phoenician alphabet had 22 signs. Like the signs of its precursors and imitators, these stood for consonants so that readers had to insert mentally most of the vowel sounds – just as readers of Arabic still do today. Otherwise it is the direct ancestor of our alphabet and of all Western scripts. It was left to the Greeks to add characters for the five vowel sounds.

COUNTING THE BOOTY Two Assyrian officials, one equipped with a writing board, the other with a scroll, make a record of captured treasure.

Sophisticated mathematics had been developed many generations before and were put to practical use in calculating compound interest and in solving engineering and survey problems in canal and construction work. There was a vibrant intellectual and scientific life. Scribe-philosophers pondered the meaning of life and mathematician-astronomers – the Einsteins of the age – grappled with complex calculations based upon centuries of observation.

NEBUCHADNEZZAR'S HANDIWORK

'I love Babylon like the apple of my eye', wrote Nebuchadnezzar, and he never ceased polishing it: strengthening defences, restoring the great ziggurat, fussing over temple improvements, even stocking a national museum. He rebuilt the Ishtar Gate three times. When he was done, the old city on the east bank of the Euphrates was wholly refurbished and protected on the land side by 6 miles (10km) of triple walls and a broad moat.

Boxed inside this by a double wall and a second moat, with towers every 20 yd (18 m) and seven gateways whose massive doors were armoured in bronze, the inner city was a fortified island within a fortified island. A bridge spanning the Euphrates connected it with a west-bank 'new city' laid out with gardens and temples, also walled and moated.

Like Sennacherib's Nineveh, streets were laid out on a cross-grid system that was quite alien to the usual higgledy-piggledy tradition; thoroughfares slanted from northeast to south-west to catch the prevailing wind and provide some relief from heat and smells. The main avenue was called Victory Way, while others were named after the gods: Marduk Street, Enlil Street, Sin Street and so on.

LAND RECORDS Symbols of the gods – for example, the eight-pointed star of Ishtar at the top – are carved on a Babylonian 'boundary stone' recording the land dealings of a soldier called Ritti-Marduk.

The city's ethnic mix was as diverse as any in the ancient world. The Judaeans found themselves rubbing shoulders with Chaldeans, Elamites, Hittites, Assyrians, Hurrians, Phoenicians, Aramaeans and the occasional Egyptian.

Socially the population was split four ways, between free and enslaved, and between temple personnel and laity. But this hid a great variety of circumstances: slaves serving a wealthy household, for instance, were likely to live in far better circumstances than a free but poor family. Some rich families owned more than 100 slaves; a typical household had two or three.

INTO THE DIASPORA

The Judaean exiles became an integral part of the Babylonian way of life – as is confirmed by both Biblical and Babylonian texts. From the start they enjoyed limited freedom to earn a living and to settle their own quarter in the city and a number rose to prominence. The prophet Jeremiah, who stayed in Judah but enjoyed Nebuchadnezzar's favour, invoked 'the Lord of Hosts, the God of Israel' in urging his exiled compatriots in a letter to settle down and accept Babylonian ways: 'Build houses and plant gardens . . . take wives and have sons and daughters, and take wives for your sons and give your daughters to husbands . . . seek the welfare of the city.'

Tablets have been found listing food subsidies issued to some members of the Judaean aristocracy. Included on the list is Jehoiachin, captured as a boy king and brought to Babylon with his brothers and mother in 597 BC. This last royal heir of the House of David spent the rest of his days at the Babylonian court.

From Babylon, trusted Judaeans were settled in a string of captured Arabian oases, where 1000 years later the faith of their descendants profoundly influenced the founder-prophet of Islam, the trader Mohammed. For the rest, their increasingly benign bondage was to last 48 years, at the end of which Babylon fell to the Persians, who gave all expatriate groups the option of returning home with their goods and gods.

A sufficient number took the offer for Jerusalem to rise once more, this time as a provincial capital in the Persian empire, but many families who had

'I WANT NO FUSS . . . KILL THEM'

MIGHTY FALLEN   An Assyrian relief shows Elamite kings reduced to the status of servants at the court of Nineveh.

IT WAS A COMMON PRACTICE for overlords or conquerors to hold as hostages members of subject royal families. Usually hostage nobility were well treated, but a change in the political climate could seal their fate. Shamsi-adad, an early king of Assyria, sent these blunt instructions to his son, Yasmah, about 1780 BC when Yasmah was running the vassal state of Mari.

❝ I had you keep the sons of Vilanum with you against the possibility of eventually making a treaty with them.

Now that I'm certain it will never come to that, have them arrested and put to death that same night. I want no fuss and no mourning. Just prepare their graves, kill them, and bury them.

Keep their head-ornaments, their clothes and their gold, and then send me their wives. You can keep the two musicians for yourself, but have Sammetar's maid brought to me. ❞

prospered chose to remain in what was now their home. The Judaeans, or Jews as they came to be known, proved themselves loyal subjects of the Persians, providing the troops for an imperial garrison at a key point on the Nile.

By the late 4th century BC, when the conquests of Alexander the Great had replaced Persian rule with Greek, people of Israelite descent had spread far and wide. What would come to be called the Diaspora was well under way.

TRADE, VENTURES AND VOYAGERS

Trains of pack donkeys made their way along valleys and through mountain passes;

sturdy trading vessels plied the rivers and seas. The merchants of the ancient Near East

traded in all manner of goods from timber to slaves, dyed cloth to gold and lapis lazuli.

FROM well before the time of Abraham in the 18th century BC, the Near East was linked from end to end, and beyond, by trade. From the Mesopotamian river cities, including Ur, Nineveh and Babylon, trade routes radiated up tributaries of the Tigris towards Afghanistan, down the Persian Gulf to Arabia, up the Euphrates to Asia Minor and – Abraham's route – through Syria to the Levant and Egypt.

Without metals or stone for building and with hardly any wood of their own, the Mesopotamians relied on trade as their lifeblood. It stimulated the creative skills of their craftsmen who fashioned imported metals and other materials into precious goods that could be exchanged for further raw materials. It also played its part in the development of lawmaking. Rates of exchange and of boat hire preceded everything else in law codes dating from 800 years before the laws of Moses.

Trade records survive from the days of Sargon, whose Mesopotamian trading empire about 2300 BC was based on Akkad, a jostling river port where goods were exchanged from as far afield as India. The link was Dilmun – modern Bahrein – an island in the Arabian Gulf that as a Bronze Age Singapore was

TREE FELLING A relief from Karnak shows princes from Lebanon felling cedar trees that will be paid in tribute to the Egyptian crown.

a bazaar of exotic items such as ivory, coral, copper vessels, eye-paints, spices and ointments. For the Mesopotamians, Dilmun's remoteness and bountifulness were such that it came to be associated in folk tales with paradise.

SNAKING LOGS AND STRINGS OF DONKEYS

Logs were sluiced down the Euphrates and provided the basis of big-scale traffic. Rafted together and buoyed on inflated hides they were a precious commodity in their own right and also bore downriver heavy loads of metal ores. The Euphrates was then known as the Urudu, the copper river, for all the ore it carried.

Overland journeys were as arduous as they were hazardous. Carts hauled by oxen were cumbersome, and, in the absence of surfaced roads, unsuitable for long-distance journeys. The solution was the pack-donkey. These resolute, sure-footed little beasts could carry loads of more than 200 lb (90 kg) in panniers slung on either side and over their backs. They typically covered 10 to 15 miles (16 to 24 km) per day.

Trails meandered according to the lie of the land and access to ferries or fords across rivers; deserts were barriers which forced detours of hundreds of miles. Wadis – dry valleys where subsoil water collects from occasional flash-flood downpours – afforded passage through some arid regions, while the major mountain passes were strategic choke-points to be controlled at all costs. South of Tyre in southern Lebanon, the gap between mountain and sea is so narrow that a 6 ft (1.8 m) trench worn into the rock face still defines the path the caravans once took.

Conducting business under such conditions was often difficult. Aside from safe, dependable transport, a merchant needed trustworthy agents and an understanding with each ruler along his line of

LOGS ON THE RIVER An Assyrian relief depicts a busy river scene with ships towing and manoeuvring logs.

trade. Trade was initially controlled by the temple authorities whose estates produced most of the goods, but even by Abraham's time private enterprises had foreign 'branch offices' and Mesopotamian states maintained courier services for business as well as official dispatches. Clay tablet manifests accompanied consignments, which were sealed against pilferage.

Deals were complicated by the absence of a currency. Coinage did not come into general use until the 5th century BC. Trade was by barter: so much of this for so much of that. Comparative values were at first quoted in terms of barley, but the commonest precious metal – silver – proved more practical.

HEAVY HAULER
Ox-carts, such as this one cast in bronze in the 12th century BC, were good for short-distance haulage.

Merchant guilds established rules to ensure their members' integrity. Credit was available for ventures at agreed rates of interest, with merchants issuing tablets of credit payable on demand by their agents. A venture contract might typically guarantee, say, a specified return in copper for a capital investment in sesame oil, wool and clothing, all valued in terms of silver. In this way merchants of the 2nd millennium BC moved large tonnages of copper over great distances as well as substantial quantities of prized rarities like lapis lazuli. Successful merchants grew rich and came to enjoy a status second only to that of royalty, whose patronage was virtually indispensable. Monarchs charged for 'visas' along the Euphrates, while elsewhere a royal letter of introduction smoothed paths.

At the private level, business arrangements could become extremely confusing. Terms were agreed in silver, but payment was made in an assortment of garments and pieces of cloth, plus some bronze pots contributed by the neighbours. Like clothes and jewellery, utensils became a kind of local currency, with each family presumably maintaining a debit and credit balance.

Sharp practice could occur at every level. A case is known of an Assyrian prince who paid for a pair

PHOENICIAN IMPORT-EXPORT Harbourside workers at Tyre unload ingots of imported copper (opposite, below).

of prize horses with 25 lb (11 kg) of lead. The weight was right, but it should have been in silver. 'What you have done is unspeakable,' the duped seller remonstrated, but the outcome is not known.

'CROCODILES OF THE WAYSIDE'

As with trade, rulers tried to control travel as much as possible. Always wary of dissidents fomenting insurrection from abroad, they sought to ensure the repatriation of fugitives by reciprocal treaty arrangements. Even desert nomads were not entirely free to roam. 'We have completed passing the Shashu

tribes of Edom through to the water holes,' states a routine report from Egyptian guards at a Sinai border post in 1204 BC. The Egyptian authorities permitted strictly supervised passage on specified dates only. They had reason to be cautious, for nomads were to them 'crocodiles of the wayside' – lurking there, ready to devour unwary passers-by.

Rulers were themselves enthusiastic traders, dealing directly with one another. Royal exchanges of gifts were an important element of diplomacy, with giver and receiver keeping a vigilant eye on the comparative value of their 'presents'.

BEADS FOR FIGURINES Israelite villagers squat in the shade of a tree as they barter goods with a visiting stranger.

One consignment from Pharaoh Akhenaton to a king in Babylon around 1370 BC consisted of more than 300 items, from beds to chariots, whose gold content alone totalled ½ ton. 'Just as you and my father were on good terms, so let it be between us,' the Babylonian king had earlier proposed. 'Whatever you want, write to me and I will have it sent to you, and whatever I want, let me write to you.' Akhenaton dispatched three ebony beds, six chairs and a headrest, all inlaid with gold and ivory 'as a present for the [Babylonian king's] new palace' and included an inventory of the gold and silver content.

The king, however, had made it clear that he wanted gold – 'much fine gold' – and he was not about to be short-changed. He dismantled everything, weighed the gold, and determined it to be less than appeared on the manifest. The consignment must have been tampered with, he coyly suggested to the pharaoh: 'Let my brother keep a close personal eye on the gold he sends. Let him seal it and send it himself.' He sent by return a meagre amount of lapis lazuli and five teams of chariot horses 'as an interim present', using as an excuse dangerous road conditions and hot weather, but promising 'many fine presents' later, presumably once the pharaoh had proved more generous.

ISRAELITES AT THE CROSSROADS

The prosperity of the Israelites was tied to their ability to control and exploit two trunk routes. The Way of the Sea from Egypt hugged the Philistine-controlled coast, then struck inland through the strategic Megiddo Pass before splitting in two, one track forking north-west to the Phoenician coast and Anatolia and the other continuing to Damascus and eventually Babylon. The King's Highway, the second key artery, struck south from Damascus through Ammon, Moab and Edom in modern

Jordan to the head of the Red Sea: this was the route taken by the incense caravans coming from south Arabia. Sometimes by force of arms the Israelites were able to control it.

King Solomon, the quintessential Biblical entrepreneur, is credited with cornering the regional horse and chariot trade by importing for resale chariots from Egypt and horses from the southern part of Turkey. The exchange rate worked out at four horses to one chariot.

Solomon also dealt with the seafaring Phoenicians. His realms reached as far as the top of the Gulf of Aqaba, and he is credited in the Bible with having them fit out and man a Red Sea merchant fleet on his behalf. This made excellent sense for the Phoenicians, who were able in this way to outflank the Egyptians. The Biblical land of Ophir, the fleet's destination, has not been identified, but on the basis of the duration of the voyages and the exotic goods brought back – gold, silver, precious stones, tropical hardwood, peacocks and apes – it might have been Somalia or possibly Suppara near Bombay.

TIPPING THE SCALES **An Egyptian carefully weighs ingots of gold.**

THE PHOENICIAN PHENOMENON

The arrangement did not last long, but that mattered little to the Phoenicians who were beginning a maritime expansion that would make them the dominant Mediterranean sea power for seven centuries. They were a loose-knit confederation of port cities

HEAD WEIGHT
A metalsmith from Canaanite Ugarit probably used this head as a weight for his scales.

dotted along a narrow seaboard, walled in behind by mountains, that corresponded roughly to modern Lebanon. They turned this trap into a springboard by adroit alliances with the major powers of the time. Their only natural assets were the timber of their mountain slopes and the purple dye they extracted from sea snails, but by reaching out with increasing daring in search of more markets, they not only multiplied their trading profits but established all kinds of domestic industries to process and craft the raw materials they shipped home.

Improvers rather than inventors, with a keen marketing sense, they learned and adapted the best technologies of the age . . . carved ivories for the Israelite, Assyrian and Aramaean courts, expensive finished textiles and gold, silver and bronzeware for the Mediterranean trade, coffins for Egypt, ships for everywhere. In the process they enriched all Near Eastern culture while enriching themselves.

Ports such as Tyre, Sidon, Byblos and Arvad were small, but an indented coastline augmented by numerous inshore islands and reefs made for

BEARING INCENSE **A camel caravan makes its way along the King's Highway, leading from Damascus to the Red Sea.**

secure anchorages. Tyre – 'haughty Tyre', the prophet Isaiah called it – was the best situated of all: a secure island bastion a few hundred yards offshore with two harbours, north and south. The population, which may have reached 50 000, was packed in crowded prosperity into humankind's first tenements. Tyre's water system was the talk of the ancient world. Spring water flowed down a conduit from the mountains, then a pulley system of tankers hauled it to the island, where an emergency reserve was stored in cisterns.

Without compass or chart, the Phoenicians voyaged as much as possible by daylight, navigating by promontory and mountain peak and the course of the sun, depending as much upon oar as their

stubby sails and anchoring or beaching overnight, or during stormy weather. For this they required safe havens around the Mediterranean and into the Black Sea; close to a hundred of these bases have been identified by archaeologists.

Piracy was endemic and as much a menace as the sudden ferocity of Mediterranean storms. From 1400 BC the pharaohs ran a coastguard service that patrolled the approaches to the Nile delta to curb smuggling and piracy, while Phoenician merchantmen of any size carried a complement of marines.

For major voyages, the Phoenicians developed a sleek craft with a curved, raised stern and a projecting prow that in an emergency served as a ram. One destination for such voyages was Tarshish, probably in modern Spain, from where they obtained silver, iron, lead and tin. Phoenician ships were equipped with two banks of oars and a short mast carrying a square sail. For local coastal trade, squatter vessels with copious holds were substituted.

Around 600 BC, under contract to Pharaoh Necho, a Phoenician crew circumnavigated Africa, sailing down the Red Sea and following the coastline all the way around to return by the Straits of Gibraltar. This greatest voyage of ancient times took three years and would not be repeated for another 2000 years. By 450 BC the Phoenicians were trading up the Atlantic seaboard as far as Brittany and may also have reached the British Isles, attracted by Cornish tin.

MIGHTY CHARGER An Assyrian groom leads out two horses.

TRADING WITHOUT MONEY IN BIBLE TIMES

MONEY as we know it did not begin to appear until the 7th century BC; the first major currency was not minted until shortly before 500 BC. Until then, all business was based upon barter and people were paid and taxed in commodities such as barley and livestock, wine and beer.

Abraham was 'very rich in cattle, in silver and in gold'. This Biblical reference accords with a time of transition from nomadic to settled life, when precious metals and copper became a less cumbersome way to measure comparative values of livestock, grain and so forth. Silver proved particularly useful, being more common than gold and easy to carry around in a bag: pieces could be snipped off a bar, weighed and exchanged for goods.

Weights and scales abounded and so did abuse, since the purity of precious metal was inconsistent – scales, too, could be rigged. There are repeated Biblical injunctions against the 'bagful of deceitful weights' and similar cheating. Setting and maintaining standards of honesty was a royal responsibility.

The basic unit everywhere in the Near East, except in Egypt, was the shekel, from a Semitic word that meant to weigh, but its value varied from state to state, even city to city. The standard Israelite shekel was about $^2/_5$ oz (11 g). Sixty shekels equalled one mina and 3600 shekels made a talent ('load'), about 75 lb (34 kg). The tiniest weight was a gerah; at one-twentieth of a shekel, it was useful in apportioning costly spices and came from an old Mesopotamian word meaning a grain of carob seed.

Foodstuffs were measured by volume rather than weight. Ten omers ('sheaves') made an ephah

MONEY WEIGHTS This silver half shekel comes from Sidon. Originally the shekel was a weight.

and ten ephahs a homer ('donkey load'). A bath was a liquid ephah. Ten baths made a kor, probably about 50 gallons (230 litres).

Coinage – the idea of using trading weights as currency – evolved in stages. By 700 BC the Assyrian king Sennacherib was casting half-shekel bronze pieces from clay moulds. The invention of the first true coinage is credited to the little kingdom of Lydia in the north of modern Turkey. Lydia was rich in electrum, a natural alloy of gold and silver found in river sand, and by 600 BC the Lydians were stamping uniform lumps of electrum with a royal seal as an official medium of trade. By 550 BC King Croesus of Lydia, whose name remains synonymous with fabulous wealth, was issuing the first silver and gold coins at an exchange rate of 20 silver coins to a single gold one.

After the Persians conquered Lydia they adopted the system for their empire. From about 512 BC Darius the Great was issuing gold and silver coins, stamped with his warrior image, as standard currency accepted from Europe to India.

STURDY TRADER For short-distance trade the Phoenicians built tubby vessels with large holds. They were black, covered all over with pitch to make them watertight.

Phoenician success showed the advantages of safer and cheaper sea commerce. On the other hand, the balance had also been redressed to some extent in favour of land trade with the introduction of the camel, domesticated in Arabia shortly before the time of Solomon. Whereas donkeys required daily watering, camels could go five days between drinks and up to three weeks in an emergency. A single beast could carry a 600 lb (270 kg) load, and charge like a war horse if the need arose. The camel caravan revolutionised lines of communication, shortening existing trails and opening new ones such as the trans-Arabian spice route.

TRADE FOLLOWS CONQUEST

Ever-uncertain security and poor to non-existent roads meant that further advances depended upon the growth of larger and more powerful empires. For the Israelites this brought opportunity and danger in equal measure. In filling a power vacuum that had existed since 1200 BC, the rampaging Assyrian armies of the 8th century BC brought a trade boom in their bloody path. The military roads they cut through their expanding empire speeded the transport of goods, while economic integration forced by the sword was accompanied by a free-trade policy.

Standards of living improved and Jerusalem experienced an explosive growth. New markets opened up for Judaean wheat, olive oil, pottery and

perfume. Phoenician trade similarly peaked in the 8th and early 7th centuries BC. And as goods from the Near East reached markets in Europe, thanks to the Phoenician traders, so Greek wine, dried fish and iron goods flowed back into the Near East. The Arabian caravan trade, protected from desert brigands by Assyrian forces, also boomed.

The Babylonian conquest of Assyria followed by the Persian conquest of Babylon – all within 70 years – completed the process of opening up vast new trade routes. Under the Persians, the Near East was united for the first time by a network of highways to speed transport and tribute from its farthest corners.

Most famous was the 1677 mile (2699 km) Royal Road from Sardis in western Turkey to Susa in the eastern foothills above the head of the Arabian Gulf. Constantly patrolled and maintained, its compacted earth surface was paved where necessary and ferries served every river crossing. Fortress checkpoints weeded out unwelcome travellers and more than 100 caravanserais – inns built around large courtyards suitable for accommodating entire

THE CODE OF THE COURIERS

The Persians had the world's first express mail service. Couriers sped along the empire's roads changing horses every 15 miles (24 km), much like the pony express of the American West 2500 years later. 'Nothing stops these couriers from covering their allotted stage in the shortest time possible – neither snow, rain, heat nor darkness', wrote the Greek historian Herodotus. An inscription on New York's General Post Office is based on these words: 'Neither snow nor rain nor heat nor gloom of night stays these couriers from the swift completion of their appointed round.'

'THIEVES HAVE STOLEN YOUR CLOTHES'

A WRY COMMENTARY on the perils of travel in 1200 BC is contained in a papyrus manuscript in the British Museum. The 'hero' of the account is an Egyptian courier who is dispatched from his native country on official business to Joppa (Jaffa, part of modern Tel Aviv).

He sets out full of bravado. His light chariot is hitched to a horse 'swift as a jackal'; his mind is filled with instructions and warnings about crossing the river Jordan and avoiding danger spots. But after only a day's travel his confidence is as shaken as his body:

❝ You halt for the evening, crushed and battered, sore in every limb. You wake early to find yourself alone. Thieves have stolen your clothes and your groom has fled with the rest of your possessions. You tug at your ear.'

Fighting rising panic, he presses on until he comes to a densely wooded ravine he fancies must be 4000 ft (1220 m) deep and teeming with bandits – 'all nine feet (2.7 m) tall and ferocious besides: not the sort you can sweet-talk.

'You then decide to go forward,' he continues, 'shuddering, hair standing on end and heart in your mouth. The path is overgrown and so precipitous that the chariot tilts on its side. Half way through you have to unfasten the yoke to repair the harness: you don't know how to do it properly. You break into a trot and eventually the sky opens and you are in the clear, but trembling again seizes you for now you are exposed and crave the protective bushes.'

The hapless courier finally reaches the outskirts of Joppa, his destination on the Mediterranean coast, where the meadows are in bloom and he finds a pretty girl watching over a vineyard:

'She welcomes you and grants you delightful favours, but you are caught together and made to hand over your shirt of finest Egyptian linen. You are worn out and fall into a deep sleep. They steal your bow, your dagger and your quiver. Your horse bolts over slippery ground and smashes the chariot to pieces.

' "I have arrived safely!" you report at headquarters. "Give me food and water." But nobody seems to hear you or pay the slightest attention to your story. ❞

PERILS OF TRAVEL Thieves make off with an unwary traveller's weapons.

TWO-TIER ROWERS Biremes were designed for long voyages. This one is a warship with a beak for ramming.

caravans – provided safe and comfortable night halts. Branch routes reached to Egypt and to India.

The consequent upsurge in international trade was stimulated further by a uniform system of weights and measures and a common currency with coins replacing the barter systems. It became more and more practical and profitable to transport basic commodities like fodder, cheap sandals and mass-produced pottery in bulk over long distances. With greater abundance came greater choice. Rice from India was introduced into Mesopotamia at this time, and Mesopotamian sesame into Egypt.

WENAMON'S PERILOUS VOYAGE TO PHOENICIA

WENAMON was an Egyptian temple official dispatched to Phoenicia in the 11th century BC to purchase timber for a barge for the sun-god Amon-Re. The story of his voyage survives as evidence of the hazards of such expeditions.

His destination was Byblos, north of Beirut, but the ship called at Dor (south of Haifa) and there a crewman made off with the jars containing his capital – more than 1 lb (450 g) of gold and 7 lb (3.2 kg) of silver. Dor was then controlled by the Tjekker, a seafaring people allied to the Philistines.

When Wenamon failed to cajole the Tjekker ruler into covering the loss until the culprit was found, he sailed on to the Phoenician city of Tyre, then Byblos. On the way, he pirated some silver from a Tjekker ship and hid it in an image of Amon-Re which he carried with him.

This enraged the Tjekker and alarmed Zakarbaal, Prince of Byblos, who was trapped between fears of Tjekker reprisal and respect due the emissary of the sun-god. Each day for five months, Zakarbaal urged his unwelcome guest: 'Go away! Get out of my harbour!' Wenamon refused to budge.

Eventually, a compromise was reached. The Phoenicians shipped off the keel for the barge and a few timbers with a message from Wenamon begging for more funds. In due course these arrived and Zakarbaal had the balance of the timber delivered. But he also tipped off the Tjekker, making a cynical deal with them: he could not arrest the envoy of such a powerful god, he said, 'but I can't stop you chasing him'.

Wenamon's crew managed to slip out of Byblos, but a storm drove them off course and when they made landfall in Cyprus, Wenamon was almost lynched by hostile locals. He managed to secure protection for himself and the crew by arguing that the Phoenicians would be sure to exact retribution on Cypriot merchants if anything happened to them.

The story does not relate if Wenamon and his cargo eventually reached safe haven. It they did, they were more than two years overdue.

THE DIVINE LAW OF KINGS

Every nation had its laws and customs handed down from generation to generation. These were

often set, literally, in stone – as with the code of Hammurabi, an 18th-century BC King of Babylon.

Among them were the laws of the Israelites, recorded in the first books of the Bible.

DISPENSING JUSTICE was a function of the ruler acting on behalf of his gods, the ultimate arbiters of all human conduct. As the gods' representative on earth, a ruler was at pains to stress highmindedness and concern for his people's well-being.

This was given dramatic expression in the case of the Assyrian and Babylonian kings, who once a year were stripped of their regalia and led before a golden image of their national god. The king was slapped about the ears and made to crouch before the idol and swear his innocence from sin. He was then given an absolution by the high priest, who smacked him once more and if the blow was hard enough to draw tears all the better, for this was considered a good omen.

Scholars once believed the Biblical laws to be the world's earliest, until the discovery in 1901 of a black stone column bearing the law code of Hammurabi. He ruled in Babylon around the time of Abraham, many hundred years before Moses. Fragments of still earlier Mesopotamian codes were subsequently unearthed. The earliest bears some of the laws of a king who ruled Ur about 2050 BC. On the reverse side the king set out his credentials as the earthly representative of the moon-god and laid claim to making reforms to ensure that 'the orphan did not fall prey to the wealthy . . . the widow to the powerful . . . the poor man to the rich'.

Hammurabi's 8 ft (2.4 m) column is engraved with 282 laws. In a prologue: 'Hammurabi, the devout, god-fearing prince' vowed 'to promote the welfare of the people, to cause justice to prevail in the land, to destroy the wicked and the evil, that the strong might not oppress the weak . . .'.

The laws of the Israelites tumble from the Hebrew Bible in exuberant confusion, the Covenant of Moses (Ten Commandments) supplemented by many particular – sometimes peculiar – measures that reveal an evolving process of lawmaking. In one instance, an injunction against the use of fake weights is juxtaposed with a measure against wives becoming carried away in helping their husbands in a fight. The wife, for grabbing the adversary between the legs, could have her hand amputated – the only law in the Old Testament that prescribes bodily mutilation as a punishment.

HARSH CODE OF THE DESERT

The laws of Moses and Hammurabi contain some striking parallels and share in some instances the principle of direct vengeance – an eye for an eye and a tooth for a tooth. Hammurabi's immediate ancestors were Amorite nomads and their harsh code, like that of the Hebrew Bible, harked back to a rigorous tradition of desert justice.

Patterns often changed as societies became more settled. The Hittites living in the region of modern Syria initially punished beehive thieves by exposing them to bee stings, but by 1600 BC had substituted this with a fine. The early Hittite farmer found guilty of breaking a religious taboo was torn limb-from-limb by teams of oxen, but this gruesome death penalty was later scrapped in favour of the symbolic dismembering of a sheep in place of the culprit

GIFTS OF THE GODS
The Sumerian monarch Ur-Nammu receives the attributes of kingship from the gods.

GODS AND THE LAW King Hammurabi of Babylon worships the sun god Shamash, also god of justice. Beneath is inscribed Hammurabi's code of laws.

and a fine of bread and beer. The Hittites went so far as to let murderers go free if they richly compensated the victim's family – a provision that favoured wealthy offenders who could afford to pay the compensation. The death penalty was mandatory only for defiance of royal authority, bestiality and rape.

In all communities, social stability counted above individual rights, and this was bolstered by an abiding fear of upsetting the gods through disturbing the established social order. This led to

guilt by association. A man's misdeeds could bring punishment upon his whole family, who might be wiped out in cases involving defiance of the ruler. Blood feuds were a closely related phenomenon and common enough among the early Israelites for refuges to be established where a man fleeing the vengeance of a clan or family could find sanctuary until his case was heard by the local elders. By grasping the corners of an altar, a temporary amnesty was assured.

The earliest courtroom was the circular open space of the village threshing floor. In urban communities, the elders – senior family heads and property-owners – settled disputes by the city gate. There were no lawyers and no cross-examination as we know it. The procedure was for the court to hear statements from accuser, accused and any witnesses, all bound by oath to the gods.

If the evidence was conflicting, there was the option of trial by ordeal: along the Euphrates, the accused was sometimes thrown in the river and abandoned to a sink-or-swim judgment of the gods. Punishment was immediate and public. Imprisonment was rare, a flogging being the usual penalty. Stoning was the most common form of execution.

Oath-taking was charged with as much religious as legal significance and the consequences of violating an oath were clearly stated. 'Lest my right hand wither,' was an old Canaanite expression that finds

VENGEANCE, OR AN EYE FOR AN EYE

LAW CODES set down on tablets by Mesopotamian kings of the early 2nd millennium BC contain many fascinating parallels with the Biblical laws of Exodus, Leviticus and Deuteronomy.

Each king professed to be acting upon the instruction of his gods. The most famous instance is that of Hammurabi of Babylon, who about 1750 BC promulgated a complex set of legal guidelines for civil and criminal cases of every description.

Babylon at that point had a class system and this was reflected in its laws with their reference to the rights and duties of 'gentlemen'. But otherwise the penalties Hammurabi prescribed for violent crime anticipated the Biblical code of 'life for life, eye for eye, tooth for tooth'. Clauses 196, 197, 200, 209 and 210 of the Hammurabi code state:

If a gentleman destroys the eye of an aristocrat, they shall destroy his eye.

If a gentleman fractures another gentleman's bone, they shall fracture his bone.

If a gentleman knocks out the tooth of another gentleman, they shall knock out his tooth.

If a gentleman strikes another gentleman's daughter and causes her to have a miscarriage, he shall pay ten shekels of silver.

If the woman dies, they shall put to death his daughter.

its way into the Bible. Fears of divine retribution stayed the tongues of perjurers, who faced possible execution if the accused was vindicated.

'I Am The Dust Of Thy Feet'

Kings were in theory answerable only to their gods and demanded appropriately abject respect. 'Who is the dog that does not obey his lord, the son of the sun?' a Canaanite prince would address the Egyptian pharaoh, continuing: 'The king, my lord, my sun, the sun in heaven, I am the dust of thy feet. Seven times seven I prostrate myself on belly and back.'

But no throne was a sinecure; kings were busy people. Records discovered at Mari, a state that flourished from about 3000 BC on the middle Euphrates, reveal intimate details of day-to-day court life that serve as a model for the responsibilities of kingship. The kings of Mari ruled a riverside nation of perhaps 100 000 people from a 300 room palace that covered several acres. This was the nation's administrative, business, military and religious hub; satellite palaces in other towns handled local affairs. Much the same system was adopted centuries later by the Israelite kings and on a grander scale by the Assyrians and Persians.

The king of Mari was a hands-on monarch. A cargo of grain bound for the palace had gone aground; a town wall was collapsing; a chariot borrowed from the palace had broken down; a fatted ox destined for the royal table had become so fat that it could not be budged: on each occasion came the plea, 'Let

FINDING SANCTUARY An Israelite pursued by enemies clutches an altar. His foes will have to leave him until their case against him has been heard by local elders.

my lord send instructions'. Israelite kings in the 1st millennium BC would carry a similar burden, as is evident from the prayer of Solomon to 'give thy servant an understanding heart'.

The gods, too, made their demands, their priests directing the king on a rigorous round of religious ritual. Dagon was the national god of Mari: a priest had only to announce that 'Dagon has sent me a message' to have the king's immediate attention.

But deference to the gods was no panacea for a weak monarchy. At least eight kings of the northern kingdom of Israel were assassinated and nine different families occupied the throne in the space of 200 years. Unlike its sister kingdom to the south, Israel lacked the central focus of Jerusalem and Judah's royal house of David. As a result, the proclamations of prophets weighed heavily in the selection of its kings and this led to murderous power struggles.

The Assyrian monarchs at their height were a complex mix of the cultured and fratricidal. Aesthetic but cruel, Sennacherib was assassinated in 680 BC in a palace coup, evidently engineered by two of his sons. A third son, Esarhaddon, secured the throne, but his death was followed in turn by a struggle

KING AT PRAYER Monarchs, such as Hammurabi here, were believed to stand in a special relationship with the gods.

between his sons. The loser immolated himself in his burning palace. The victor, Ashurbanipal, 'tore out the tongues of those whose slanderous mouths had uttered blasphemies against my god Ashur' – and after a mass slaughter of the rival faction, he embarked upon a long reign which was remarkable for its prosperity and scholarly endeavour. Throughout these struggles, in which Babylon was twice sacked, all sides claimed to have the support of the gods, who were consulted at every turn.

INTERNATIONAL RELATIONS

International law was a matter between kings, who addressed one another as 'brother', 'father' or 'son', according to their relative might. This could lead to testy exchanges. 'Are you implying that we were born of the same mother? Don't talk brotherhood with me', a Hittite king scolded an early Assyrian monarch who had presumed too much. Royal messengers – ambassadors – represented kings at foreign courts where they were protected by traditions of hospitality to travellers, although they might be held up for years if relations soured.

Just as royal daughters were prized war booty, dynastic marriages were important in sealing alliances. Judah and Israel tried to patch up their differences in this way. They also sought to strengthen their ties with the Phoenicians with dynastic alliances – the infamous Jezebel, wife of Ahab, King of Israel, was a Tyrian princess.

For all their bellicosity, Near Eastern rulers appreciated the benefits of peace, even if they much preferred it to be on their own terms. Of the achievement of the Assyrian Ashurbanipal, it was said that 'throughout all lands a peace prevailed. Like finest oil were the world's four quarters'.

Oaths of loyalty were effective in binding a vassal ruler to the terms of a treaty: he was anointed on his head with oil and water and required to swear by his own gods, who were appointed the wreakers of vengeance in the event of default. Vassals lost their right to an independent foreign policy and sometimes suffered trade restrictions. They also had to pay an annual tribute, but in return they were afforded protection. In a Biblical example, when King Ahaz of Judah sent envoys to the Assyrian monarch Tiglath-pileser III saying 'I am thy servant and thy son: come up and save me out of the hand of the King of Syria and out of the hand of the King of Israel', Tiglath-pileser duly obliged and Judah survived while Israel did not.

DIVINE WITNESS A Babylonian 'boundary stone' records land transactions involving King Meli-Shipak and his daughter, witnessed by the goddess Nana.

'I CLAPPED MY HANDS TO CALL THE GODS'

ANCIENT KINGS looked to the gods for instruction and support and for the justification of their actions. Esarhaddon secured the Assyrian throne in 680 BC following the assassination in a palace coup of his father Sennacherib. This is his official account of what happened:

❛ I was the youngest brother, but my father upon the command of the gods chose me as his successor. To secure my succession, my father assembled my brothers and all his male offspring and before the people he made them take a solemn oath in the presence of the gods of Assyria and of all the other gods. . . .

But when I occupied the crown prince's palace my brothers abandoned their godliness and spread slander against me, alienating my father, even though in the depths of his heart he still loved me. I . . . appealed to Ashur, king of the gods, and to the merciful Marduk, who made me stay in a hiding place. . . .

Thereupon my brothers went out of their senses, committing all sorts of wickedness and even drawing their weapons in Nineveh itself, a violation of the will of the gods, as they butted each other like goats in a struggle for the kingship.

I, Esarhaddon, . . . became angry as a lion. I clapped my hands to call the gods, and prayed to Ashur, Sin, Shamash, Bel, Nebo and Nergal, to the Ishtar of Nineveh

GODDESS AND LION The war and fertility goddess Ishtar stands on a lion, an animal commonly associated with her. Before her is a female worshipper.

and the Ishtar of Arbela. They duly sent me this correct . . . answer by means of a trustworthy oracle: "Do not delay. We will march with you and kill your enemies."

I did not wait a single day, but with a small force I spread my wings like the storm bird and took the difficult direct route to Nineveh, unafraid of the snow and cold. My brothers' best soldiers barred the way, sharpening their weapons, but terror of the great gods seized them at the sight of my advancing force. The goddess Ishtar, the Lady of Battle, who favours me as her high priest, broke their bows and broke their formation. Upon her lofty command they came over to me in

droves, gambolling like lambs as they acknowledged me as their lord. The people of Assyria came to meet me and kissed my feet.

The usurpers deserted their troops when they heard of this and fled the country. . . .

On the favourable day of the festival of Nebo, I joyfully entered Nineveh, my capital, and sat down happily on my father's throne. At that moment the south wind blew – an excellent portent sent by the god Ea. Other favourable omens of the sky and earth followed and my confidence grew. I deemed the rebel military commanders to be collectively guilty. I exterminated their male offspring. ❜

The Israelites, even when united under one monarch, were never more than a medium-sized power and their influence was consequently limited. But as empires around them grew stronger and the judicial reach of the empires' rulers grew ever greater, the resulting aggressive imperialism had a positive effect in reducing anarchy.

The Hittites when at their peak around 1300 BC controlled an empire that stretched from the Aegean as far south as the Lebanon. Assyrian power by 700 BC extended in a 1400 mile (2250 km) arc from Egypt to the Persian Gulf, embracing for the first time all the Fertile Crescent, the crescent-shaped *continued on page 106*

A TALE OF TWO KINGS

Even under Hezekiah, one of the best of its kings,

little Judah was no match for the might of Assyria.

THE BIBLICAL writers heap high praise on Hezekiah who ruled Judah as co-regent with his father Ahaz from around 727 BC and then succeeded to the sole kingship after his father's death.

He was able, energetic and devout, a religious reformer who tore down defiling altars and hilltop shrines to foreign gods. For the author of the Book of Kings he was worthy of comparison with his ancestor King David: 'He did what was right in the eyes of the Lord, according to all that David his father had done.'

During his reign, he also faced one of the severest challenges his small kingdom had experienced – from the Assyrian Empire. This threat was brought home to him in 721, when the Assyrians sacked Samaria, capital of the northern kingdom of Israel. There was now no buffer to help to shield the southern kingdom.

Hezekiah's father Ahaz had played safe with a submissively pro-Assyrian policy. Hezekiah was more robust. Once he assumed sole kingship he set about reordering Judah's defences which included building the Siloam water tunnel to protect Jerusalem's water supplies. Then in 704 BC the Assyrian king Sargon II died and was succeeded by his son Sennacherib. The period of uncertainty that invariably accompanied such transfers of power offered Hezekiah – and other middle-ranking rulers – an opportunity to strike against the Near East's dominant power.

In the event, Hezekiah's first response was cautious. When envoys arrived from Merodach-Baladan, a rebel Babylonian prince trying to drum up allies, he refused to do a deal. A few years later, however, he was in outright confrontation with Sennacherib, having formed an alliance with neighbouring Phoenician and other kingdoms, possibly in expectation of help from Egypt.

The allied kingdoms were no match for the Assyrian war machine. One by one they fell until only Hezekiah stood out against Sennacherib in Jerusalem. Much of Judah, too, fell to the invaders, notably Lachish, from where Sennacherib dispatched senior officers to parley with the capital's stubborn defenders. 'Do not let Hezekiah deceive you', the officers shout up to the defenders in the Biblical account. 'Do not let [him] make you rely on the Lord by saying, the Lord will surely deliver us, . . . Has any of the gods of the nations ever delivered his land out of the hand of the King of Assyria? Where are the gods of Hamath and Arpad? Where are the gods of Sepharvaim, Hena and Ivvah?'

As it happened Jerusalem never did fall to the Assyrians. According to the Bible, 'the angel of the Lord went forth [at night],

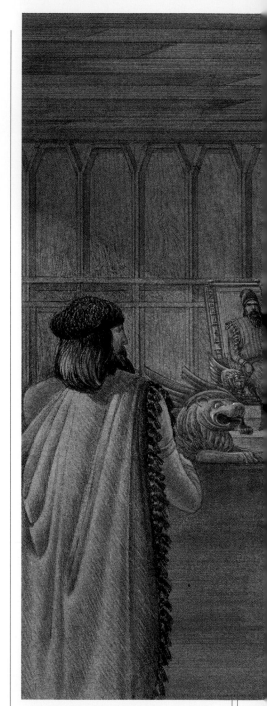

and slew 185 000 in the camp of the Assyrians', which may indicate that an outbreak of malaria or another disease forced the attackers to withdraw. It also seems likely that Hezekiah decided on discretion as a better course

COURTLY SCENE Hezekiah receives Assyrian envoys in the cedar-lined Hall of Justice of Jerusalem's royal palace.

than continued rebellion and agreed to pay tribute to the Assyrians. 'Hezekiah himself, whom the terror-inspiring splendour of my lordship had overwhelmed,' Sennacherib noted in a chronicle of his reign, '. . . did send me, later, to Nineveh': gold, silver, precious stones, antimony, 'large cuts of red stone', ivory-inlaid couches, elephant hides, ebony wood, box wood 'and all kinds of valuable treasures', as well as 'his own daughters, concubines, male and female musicians'.

area of relatively fertile land where the Near East's earliest civilisations arose. The Persians by 500 BC controlled 2 million sq miles (5.2 million km²) from Egypt to India, ruling an estimated 10 million people.

Brute force could not hold together so vast an empire. Instead, the Persian kings pursued a policy of decentralisation under which local customs and beliefs were nourished instead of suppressed. Persian law enforcement gained a reputation for fairness reflected in contemporary references to 'the law of the Medes and Persians that may not be altered'.

No king aspired to nobler sentiments than Darius the Great. 'By the favour of [the god] Ahura Mazda I act as friend to right; I am not a friend to wrong,' he vowed. 'It is not my desire that the weak man shall be wronged by the strong, nor is it my desire that the mighty man shall be wronged by the weak. I am not a friend to the liar. I am not hot-tempered. When I find myself getting angry, I control myself. I am firmly ruling over myself.'

But his autocratic successors fell victims to their own glory. Their elaborate ceremonials increasingly separated them from lesser mortals, among whom only members of seven elite families had right of access to the royal presence. They lost touch, and eventually lost everything to the squabbling Greeks, united under their own Macedonian conqueror, Alexander the Great.

ECONOMIC RIGOURS OF THE BIBLICAL WORLD

A POWERFUL ROYAL establishment backed by military might was essential for any nation's prosperity and success. But it could also lead to gross disparities of wealth and eventual revolt.

Israelites were confronted with the conflicting demands of nation-building and social justice when Solomon overextended himself and ran up a massive debt to Tyre – for raw materials and technological aid – during his construction programme in Jerusalem. Repayment, in wheat and olive oil, was still not complete after 20 years. The population was further burdened by having to feed a bloated court.

'Solomon's glory' secured status for the Israelites, but his excesses contributed to the permanent political split between Jerusalem and the north. Two centuries later, from about 780 BC, prosperity generated by trade caused a growing crisis as better-placed members of the population bought up land and the less fortunate fell into debt. This was the

CHAIN GANGS Assyrian soldiers stand guard as gangs of prisoners use ropes and a giant lever to haul a statue from its quarry.

cue for the prophets to vent their outrage and kings in Jerusalem to attempt reforms (often reasserting ancient practices that had fallen out of use), including a welfare programme for the poor and severe curbs on property transfers.

Neither could great empires escape similar economic dislocation.

Nebuchadnezzar's wars and his building programmes put a burden on Babylon's resources. Prices rose 50 per cent in the decade after 560 BC and eventually doubled, making Persia's conquest all the simpler. The Persian Empire in turn fell apart as assets became concentrated in the hands of an indolent few.

WARFARE IN BIBLICAL TIMES

Weapons such as slings and bows were accurate and deadly when wielded by experts.

Bronze gave way to iron for making arms and armour. The horse brought a new

dynamic to battle – in the use of light horse-drawn chariots and squadrons of cavalry.

THE HEBREW BIBLE is loud with the din of battle, and the 3500-year-old mummy of an Egyptian pharaoh bears present testimony to the hacking horrors of the kind of warfare it depicts. Pharaoh Seqenenre was cut down in battle by Canaanite spear, axe and dagger. Each wound is etched deeply into his grimacing skull – he was speared in the forehead, axed in the crown and stabbed across the cheekbone.

Conquest and trade went hand in hand, for the powerful were never loath to seize what they desired by brute force. By the 2nd millennium BC, local rulers commanding armies several thousand strong went on the march whenever opportunity beckoned. 'Come quickly', wrote one minor king on the upper Euphrates to an ally of the moment. He had his eye on three towns that were poorly fortified, he explained: 'We can take them all in a day and your troops will have plenty of booty.'

As empires grew, the amount of booty they seized became greater. 'I cut down with the sword and conquered', Esarhaddon of Assyria declared in summarising a rampage through 22 states around 670 BC. Conquerors acted like jackdaws, seizing all that was eye-catching as well as the valuable and useful. An inventory of booty from a campaign waged by Tiglath-pileser III of Assyria includes 'gold, silver, tin, iron, elephant hides, ivory, linen garments with multicoloured fringes, blue-dyed wool, purple-dyed wool, ebony, boxwood, precious articles from royal treasuries, lamb hides dyed purple, birds with wings dyed blue'. Darius the Great epitomised the conquering spirit at its simplest

KINGS AT WAR Tiglath-pileser III was a notable campaigner who greatly extended the Assyrian Empire.

when he boasted in 500 BC: 'I am a Persian. I grabbed Egypt.'

Rulers justified their conduct by making conquest a religious duty and giving credit for victory to their gods: 'Enlil did not let anyone oppose Sargon', an Assyrian text asserts of the man who destroyed Israel in 722 BC. The Israelites, for their part, saw nothing outrageous in statements like this from Exodus: 'The Lord is a man of war; the Lord is his name.'

MILITARY TACTICS

A relief from about 2450 BC shows the army of Lagash, north of Ur, advancing into battle. The troops are armed with copper helmets, spears and axes, and they are formed in closed ranks, protected by a front line of men bearing large rectangular shields edge to edge – the phalanx had been invented.

SHOULDER TO SHOULDER Soldiers from the Sumerian state of Lagash move into battle in phalanx formation.

Bodies of men continued to pound one another in this way, the blows more resounding as bronze replaced copper, until around 1700 BC when the light horse chariot burst upon the scene with stunning effect. Developed by warrior societies from the steppes of Eastern Europe or Asia, it spearheaded a major assault upon the Near East. The Mesopotamians had experimented with war carts hauled by onagers (or wild asses), but the light and fleet vehicles that whirled forth from beyond the Caucasus in the skilled hands of *maryanna* – lordly charioteers who constituted the world's first knighthood – were far more deadly.

Chariot warfare reached its apogee with the Battle of Kadesh in 1301 BC, when the Hittites with

3500 chariots almost crushed Ramses II of Egypt, who fielded a similar number. Commanders subsequently learned to counter the chariot with massed infantry, supported by mounted archers to pick off the horses. Gradually cavalry replaced chariots as horse breeds improved.

The big Nisaean chargers ridden by the Medes, coming from the region of modern Turkmenistan

THE CHARIOT: ALL-PURPOSE ASSAULT WEAPON

WAR MACHINE Assyrian charioteers lash their horse. The relief, from Nineveh, records King Ashurbanipal's defeat of Elamite foes about 645 BC.

THE NIMBLE HORSE CHARIOT was the jeep, armoured car and fighter aircraft of Old Testament warfare. It revolutionised military strategy from its introduction in the 2nd millennium BC when it spurred history's first arms race.

Costly to purchase and maintain, it put a financial strain on warlike rulers who had to field hundreds of chariots requiring grooms and training and maintenance personnel. The horses for the chariots also amassed formidable fodder bills.

Chariots carried a crew of two, a driver and an archer. The Hittites added punch with a three-man combination of driver and spear-thrower along with a shield-bearer to fend off enemy missiles.

Designs were constantly improved in quest of the ideal balance of speed, strength and manoeuvrability. The vehicle was generally propelled by two horses yoked on either side of a central shaft. There was sometimes a leashed reserve animal cantering alongside.

The two wheels were large – up to 5 ft (1.5 m) in diameter. Springing was achieved by making the floor of leather thongs or laced ropes and setting the wheels as far back as possible to reduce vibration and facilitate spin turns, but it was a bumpy ride nonetheless.

Improved counter-tactics and the emergence of heavy cavalry gradually reduced the chariot's effectiveness. Attaching scythes to the wheels was tried but abandoned after a few experiments; nor did heavier protective armour for vehicle and horses prove of sufficient benefit to outweigh loss in speed.

By the Old Testament's closing era, the chariot was largely retired to ceremonial duties. The massive Persian army Xerxes sent against the Greeks in 480 BC featured only two contingents of charioteers, one Libyan and the other an Indian corps using onagers, or wild asses, instead of horses and impractical for any assault role.

FIGHTING TWO BY TWO Mounted Assyrian archers, riding bareback, fight in pairs allowing one to hand over the reins of his horse to the other while firing.

east of the Caspian Sea, made the supreme warhorses. 'The glory of his nostrils is terrible,' avers the Book of Job of such a charger. 'He smelleth the battle afar off, the thunder of the captains, and the shouting.' Cavalry units were variously armed with bow, javelin and long lance, while a unit fought for the Persians with lassos and daggers. Camels came comparatively late into the fray, ridden by pairs of nomads, one on the reins and the other firing a bow.

SPEAR, SLING AND BOW

Iron weapons – only a few at first, and the preserve of princes – displaced bronze during the 1st millennium BC. The sling remained a potent weapon, its 2 in (5 cm) stone ball deadly when hurled by an expert. The bow, in universal use in various designs, was the prime weapon of the Egyptians. The powerful composite bow of glue-bonded wood and bone, in use in Mesopotamia from the 3rd millennium BC, was accurate at 50 yd (46 m) and could kill at up to ten times that range.

The Egyptians, short of metal, were slow to develop body armour and siege technology, but their charioteer-bowmen were the best in the ancient world. Their armies were built around divisions of 5000 men, primarily recruited from a single region or temple estate.

Assyrian might was based upon the bludgeon impact of heavy infantry, supported on the flanks by light infantry, chariotry and cavalry. The light infantry were armed with bows. The heavy infantry were shock troops who fought with spear and sword and wore heavy coats with overlapping bronze or iron scales, metal greaves to protect their legs and pointed metal helmets.

The more nimble Persian armies were structured around a decimal system. A company of

100 men was known as a 'flag'; ten flags made up a regiment and ten regiments made up a division. Their cavalry, armed with bow and javelin, made wheeling attacks to soften up the enemy, while the infantry fired volleys of arrows from behind a hedge of light wicker shields. Their object was to engage in hand-to-hand fighting only when ammunition was exhausted and the enemy demoralised.

THE MERCENARY FACTOR

All armies employed mercenaries, often recruited from defeated enemies. An Egyptian force dispatched to the north on a punitive expedition shortly before 1200 BC – when a victory over the nascent Israelites is recorded – consisted of 5000

READY FOR ACTION
Israelite warriors are armed with spear, bow and sling, the standard weapons of battling armies in King David's time.

troops, of which less than half were Egyptian. The balance was made up of 1700 Libyans, 880 Sudanese and 520 Sherden, who were Viking-like sea raiders allied to the Philistines.

As foes, the Sherden had so impressed Ramses II a few years earlier that he pressed them into service as his personal bodyguard. Israelites in their turn hired Philistines. The Assyrians mustered the best elements of the armies they vanquished and even managed to recruit 50 Israelite chariot crews from among their starved victims in conquered Samaria. The Persian army of Xerxes included contingents from 45 ethnic groups, ranging from Ethiopian cavalry to Nubian long bowmen.

Few Near Eastern peoples were sailors, and some navies were entirely raised from abroad. The Assyrians knew only river navigation, using dinghy-like skin boats to ferry troops across the Euphrates. 'I washed my weapons in the Great Sea', Shalmaneser III reported with satisfaction, but that was as far as most Assyrian kings cared to venture. Warships were little more than troop transports until the development of the ram in the 1st millennium BC; until then, sea fights were grappling and boarding melees waged close inshore.

The Phoenicians, unlike most of their neighbours, were superb sailors and navigators and they also led in naval architecture. Always ready to serve the powerful, they engineered history's first amphibious assault for the Egyptians, who in 1472 BC crossed the Euphrates in prefabricated craft carted over the mountains from the Mediterranean. By the Persian era, the Phoenicians could supply 200-300 warships on demand, including state-of-the-art triremes with three banks of oars and a narrow beam for speed; each carried a crew of 200 plus 30 marines.

'WHEN KINGS GO FORTH'

The customary time to take up arms was after the spring planting – the Biblical 'time when kings go forth to battle' – just as the best time to consolidate victory was when the enemy's crops were becoming ripe for plucking.

WAR BY SEA Egyptian warships had both oars and sails. The Egyptians and Philistines fought one of the first recorded sea battles, in the 12th century BC.

From pre-Biblical times kings, whether going to battle or not, surrounded themselves with bodyguards who became the nucleus of standing armies. Israelite kings had their 'mighty men'; Sargon of Assyria never moved without his crack cavalry escort. The tradition culminated with Persia's 'Immortals', an elite guard division so-named because when one was killed he was immediately replaced.

Conscription filled out the ranks as necessary, sometimes reluctantly. Surviving reports refer to conscripts 'laughing and singing', but an instance is also known of a proposal to scare out draft-dodgers by executing one and taking his head on tour. Individuals could win exemption from military service on compassionate grounds – if they were a family's sole breadwinner, for instance – or if they were engaged in essential work. Under Israelite law, bridegrooms were granted deferment for a year.

Kings took direct command of a campaign and liked to stress their own valour. 'I personally captured the Egyptian princes,' Sennacherib of Assyria boasted, and he left a spirited description of himself on the march: 'Where the terrain was difficult I rode a horse and had my chariot carried. Where it became too steep I scrambled up on foot like a wild ox. When my knees became weary I sat down on a mountain rock and drank cold water.'

ORACLES AND SPIES

Since war was supposed to be waged at the will of the gods, their approval had first to be obtained for it. So a king would visit a shrine and prostrate himself before the image of the relevant deity while priests clapped their hands and sang lamentations to get the god's attention. Sacrifices were offered and omens sought.

'My lord heard my words of righteousness,' Sargon of Assyria reported in justifying a 714 BC campaign. 'They pleased him. He inclined to my just prayer. He agreed to my request.' Though couched in prayer, requests were bloodthirsty. 'Rip open my enemy in the fight as one rips open a bundle. Loose upon him a tempest, an evil wind,' was one typical Assyrian exhortation.

Armies travelled with priest-diviners and oracles charged with keeping in constant communication with the gods. Animal entrails and the moon and stars were studied, sacrifices once more offered and curses pronounced before important tactical decisions were taken.

Records describe how Lydian and Mede armies were once locked in battle when the midday sun darkened. The troops became so alarmed by this sign of the gods' displeasure that both sides fled the

HAND TO HAND Israelites and Philistines battle on the plain beneath a fortified city. In David's time, Israelite armies were organised by tribes, each specialising in different weapons – such as the Benjamites who 'were bowmen, and could shoot arrows and sling stones . . .'

field. Because it was a solar eclipse, scholars are able to pinpoint the battle's precise date: it was May 28, 681 BC. There was a happy ending. The heir to the Mede throne married the Lydian king's daughter to usher in a generation of peace.

Reliance upon the gods was tempered with prudence. Spies were employed, as were double agents: nomad informers working secretly for the Hittites tricked Ramses II into a near-fatal trap at Kadesh. Suspicious troop and nomad movements were watched and reported as part of a well-organised intelligence-gathering operation that was typical of Assyrian efficiency. Informers who 'opened the ears of their lords' were rewarded royally.

The Persians were masters of intrigue and deception with an empire-wide intelligence agency staffed by 'listeners'. Cyrus the Great once received a secret message stitched up in a hare and another was smuggled from the capital Susa to the Aegean coast tattooed onto the scalp of a slave.

ASSYRIANS ON THE MARCH

By Assyrian times around the 11th century BC, an imperial army on the march was an awesome sight. At its head were borne the standards of the gods, accompanied by soothsayers, diviners and other holy men. Then came the king in his chariot protected by a swarming bodyguard of young noblemen and attended by his staff officers, intelligence corps, interpreters and scribes. On either flank, forces of light infantry advanced in skirmish order as a protective shield and scout force.

Behind the royal party came the main body of the army, including contingents from every subject province, each in its distinctive national dress and equipped according to the military specialisation of its region. At the rear trundled the transports creaking under the weight of siege equipment, followed by the baggage train. Despite such encumbrances, an Assyrian army could force-march 30 miles (48 km) in a day.

The Assyrians claimed – probably with some exaggeration – to muster armies of well over 100 000 for their campaigns, but in ostentation and size they were to be outmatched by the Persians, who by the 5th century BC were marching to war under an eagle standard with a swagger never to be excelled. Eight sacred white horses drew the empty chariot of the invisible god Ahuramazda and eight more hauled the royal coach amidst a colourful host reportedly 300 000 strong and accompanied by platoons of orderlies, chefs, even perfume-makers and hundreds of pampered concubines.

The Israelite soldier was rarely so indulged. Usually, each man carried his own rations of compact, nutritious foodstuffs, such as parched corn, dried raisins, bread and cheese. Along the line of march supplies were augmented by exacting 'peace offerings' of cattle, sheep and grain from the local people.

A campaign's prime objective was generally to secure as much 'tribute' as possible at minimum cost. Usually a skirmish was sufficient to demonstrate the

BATTLE ORDER   A slingman, a spearman and two archers represent the key elements in the Assyrian army.

LADDERS UP Assyrian besiegers attack an enemy town. A defender, pierced by an arrow, falls from the walls.

might of the invasion force and terms would be agreed. If a king bolted his gates to wait it out, the invader might devastate the surrounding countryside and move on, or go for the kill by laying siege. Sennacherib in 705 BC boasted that he shut up Hezekiah in Jerusalem 'like a bird in a cage' while taking 46 lesser places 'by escalade . . . siege engines, storming on foot, by mines, tunnels and breaches'.

The siege was the great setpiece of warfare. The Greek historian Herodotus cited a siege of the Philistine city of Ashdod lasting 29 years, though he failed to explain the circumstances. Sieges of many months were the rule, and several years were quite common. Defenders had time to prepare. Arriving caravans kept citizens abreast of political developments and an approaching force had no reason to cloak its might, since that was often sufficient to induce paralysing panic and submission.

A final warning for defenders came from fire beacons, the telegraph of Old Testament times. 'We are looking for the signals of Lachish . . . we do not see Azekah': these words were scratched on a fragment of pottery by an officer at a forward observation post. They were found in the ruins of a gate-tower at the Judaean city of Lachish and may have been the last message received in the doomed city in 588 BC. Jeremiah provides Biblical collaboration by reporting that Lachish and Azekah held out longest against the Babylonian assault which ended with the destruction of Jerusalem.

The first objective upon surrounding a city was to cut off its water supply by locating and stopping up any secret source beyond the walls – typically a tunnel leading to a concealed spring. The besieged population, bloated with rural refugees, was thrown back on the finite reserves of its water cisterns and food stores.

Siege techniques were being improved all the time. Under covering fire from bow and sling, for instance, ramps were thrown up and siege machines rolled against the walls. Some of these machines had 'beaks' which were wedged between the stones of the walls; rams were then used to dislodge the stones. Some of the machines were towers from which to harry the defenders on the walls and to hook and rip down the wooden platforms from which the defenders fought.

APPALLING PRIVATIONS

Coverings of hides protected the assault crews and these had to be constantly drenched with water in order to quench the fires from torches slung down by the defenders.

Cities in high summer were highly combustible, and invaders tried to set them alight with flaming brands. Tunnelling sappers meantime dug holes under the fortifications; they shored the holes up with timber props which they then set on fire to bring down a section of wall, unless prevented from doing so by defending sappers who had got there first.

Appalling privation existed in besieged cities. Malnutrition and foul water fostered disease and

SENNACHERIB AND THE SIEGE OF LACHISH

ACCORDING TO the Biblical chronicler: 'Sennacherib himself laid siege against Lachish, and all his power with him.' The Assyrian king so relished the events of 701 BC that he decorated his palace at Nineveh with vibrant alabaster reliefs depicting them, so that today we can follow the fighting in detail.

Lachish was a Judaean town that stood on a high mound 25 miles (40 km) south-east of Jerusalem, a bastion commanding the trade route from Egypt to Mesopotamia and the Philistine border. Sennacherib encircled the city, cutting off its supply lines, and constructed a brick ramp on which to haul his lumbering siege engines up the slope to the walls. Then the battering began. Under covering fire from archers the rams thudded away, while defenders on top of the walls hurled down heavy missiles, boiling oil and firebrands. Assyrian support troops wielding ladles doused fires started by direct hits on the framework of the siege machines.

When Lachish fell, the Assyrians set about looting and burning. The dead were slung into a pit along with pig bones and other refuse of the conquering army. Prisoners who had incurred the Assyrians' wrath were impaled on poles; others were roped together and dragged off to Assyria, where the reliefs depict a wretched cavalcade on the march . . . a woman with her belongings in a bag, a boy tugging at her skirts and triumphant soldiers holding aloft gory heads.

Sennacherib staged a victory parade after the campaign and reviewed his troops from a throne set up in a pleasant palm grove. As the captive elders grovelled in submission, the Assyrian king's generals made their reports and displayed their booty.

IN THE SHADE Soldiers and prisoners parade booty before Sennacherib after his capture of Lachish in Judah.

food prices soared until there was a raging black market in the most gruesome morsels. A Biblical account of the siege of Samaria in the 9th century BC states that the price of a donkey's head reached 80 shekels (2 lb – 910 g) of silver and 'dove's dung' fetched 5 shekels (2 oz – 57 g) a pint. This was the occasion of the horrific Biblical story of two mothers who agreed to cook and eat their sons: satiated after dining upon her neighbour's child, the second mother broke the bargain by hiding her own.

115

'I AM STUCK IN THIS HELLHOLE'

DISCOMFORT AND BOREDOM broken by periods of anxiety and fear was the lot of the common soldier in Old Testament times as now. An Egyptian officer sent to a small garrison on the Lebanese coast to supervise some construction work sent this dismal letter home around 1300 BC:

❛I am stuck in this hellhole without supplies. Everything I brought is used up and I have no donkeys – they were all stolen. There's no straw in the district and anyhow I have nobody to make bricks. I spend my days birdwatching and doing a little fishing and eyeing the road home with homesick longing.

I take my siesta under trees bare of fruit, attacked by gnats and mosquitoes and sandflies that suck my blood. If ever a jug of wine is opened and people come out to get a cup, 200 large dogs and 300 jackals smell the liquor and hang around the house. The heat never lets up.'

From the same period an urgent dispatch survives from the other side. It was written by a commander named Shumiyan who was guarding passes against a threatened Egyptian expedition. His men had taken up positions in June. It was now November, and his pleas for reinforcements had gone unheeded.

He made this final appeal to his ruler in the port city of Ugarit:

'I have half my chariots deployed on the coast and half against the Lebanon mountains. I have stationed myself in the valley. The rains are falling, but we are standing fast. My men repulsed a night attack and captured one man. I interrogated [him] . . . He says: "The King of Egypt has come forth." If this is true and the king strikes quickly, I cannot hold him, but if he is sending only a limited force, we will prevail if my lord sends more troops and chariots. I prostrate myself at the feet of my lord. Do not leave me here to perish. ❜

Around 650 BC, in the final days of a three-year siege of Babylon by Ashurbanipal of Assyria, the dead were piled in the streets and survivors 'ate the flesh of their sons and daughters for their starvation', according to the victor's account. The Book of Deuteronomy renders into poetry the curse of siege warfare: 'Thou shalt eat the fruit of thine own body, the flesh of thy sons and daughters . . . in the siege.'

The climax to a siege came when defenders were too weakened to put up further resistance and the enemy poured in to sack and burn the city.

TERROR AS A WEAPON OF WAR

The Assyrians in developing the art of total war also developed the judicious use of terror as a psychological weapon. They often mixed it with peaceful overtures aimed at setting people against their commanders, who had most to fear from the enemy at the gate. Attackers trumpeted

their own ferocity by having captives impaled before an obdurate town, and they blinded, burned or flayed the most defiant of its inhabitants; then they let the rest go free to spread their terrifying accounts. Once the fugitives reached the enemy capital, the fight frequently went out of its rulers, who 'became like dead men', Sargon II contentedly reflected in 714 BC.

Despite such gory boasts, indiscriminate destruction was, in fact, the exception, and increasing attempts were made to limit war's savagery through conventions, such as the injunction in Deuteronomy, not always observed, against destroying fruit trees. But civil wars were continued cause for extremes in cruelty, such as those in the Biblical account of Israel's internal strife when King Menahem had pregnant women 'ripped up' in 745 BC.

HEAD COUNT An Assyrian warrior of the 7th century BC makes a pile of the chopped-off heads of Elamite foes.

MUSIC, SONG AND DANCE

Instruments played by the peoples of the Near East ranged from harps to pipes,

rams' horns to drums. Among the Israelites, yearly festivals included the Passover in

spring and the autumnal Feast of Ingathering celebrating the wine and olive harvests.

LIVING so much amid uncertainty – from the hazards of climate or man-made catastrophes such as war – people in Old Testament times seized on every opportunity to throw off their cares and party.

Indeed, this was so much so that the Mesopotamians assumed the same of their gods who, they believed, liked nothing better than to 'smack their tongues' and sit down to feast:

They ate and drank;
Sweet drink dispelled their disquiet.
They sang for joy, drinking
*   strong wine.*
They grew elated, with carefree hearts.

MUSIC LOVER This musical performer comes from 14th-century BC Canaan.

selves into a prophetic frenzy with pipes and lutes.

The form of the dances can be tantalisingly glimpsed in a stanza from the Bible's Song of Solomon where the writer's beloved (the Shulammite) is shown performing the 'Mahanaim dance':

Turn, turn, O Shulammite;
Turn, turn, that we may gaze
*   upon you.*
Ah, gaze on the Shulammite, in the
*   Mahanaim dance.*
How beautiful are your sandalled
*   steps,*
O rapturous maiden!

This Babylonian depiction of divine revelry is echoed by the prophet Isaiah, who put it in mortal terms: 'Joy and gladness, slaying oxen, and killing sheep, eating flesh, and drinking wine: let us eat and drink; for tomorrow we die.' Feasting and wine drinking were synonymous for the Israelites; the same word sufficed for both in their language.

MUSIC-MAKING

Old Testament times were equally alive with music, song and dance, often in exuberant combination. Every occasion, whether solemn, sad or celebratory, demanded its special musical accompaniment – feast, wedding, funeral, the return of victorious armies or a band of holy men busy working them-

Royalty and nobility took pride in the quality of the musicians and singers they had to entertain them while they dined. Eight centuries before Abraham, musicians at the court of Ur plucked superbly crafted lyres while women sang. Nearly 2000 years later, a similar scene was repeated as Ashurbanipal of Assyria and his queen dined in their palace garden. Music-making of common folk has to be imagined, but there were regular public performances in Babylon, and taverns afforded opportunity for more spontaneous expression. The Mesopotamians' mastery of mathematics led them to devise a musical scale based upon geometric progression.

Harps and lyres came in many shapes and sizes. The *kinnor*, the Biblical harp played by David, was

IN PRAISE OF VICTORY A woman musician strikes up on a lyre and a king sips from a bowl as he celebrates triumph in war.

a small, handheld instrument. The *nebal* ('psaltery') had a rounded sound box like a lute. There was a wide choice of percussion instruments, from the big bass drum to the *tof* (timbrel or tambourine) tapped by women to set the tempo to song and dance. The *halil* (pipe) was bored out of wood, cane or bone and had a reed in the mouthpiece. The *geren* (cornet) was made from an animal horn, much like the *shofar*, a ram's horn. A harsh-toned metal trumpet, long and straight, was the principal instrument of war.

Music was crucial in religious rituals. In Mesopotamia the harp was regarded as a divine invention. Flute-playing echoed from temple forecourts and huge kettledrums beaten by a pair of priests, and sometimes accompanied by the blowing of bulls' horns, produced a roar known as 'full music' that reverberated throughout a city.

SWEET MUSIC This female harpist was employed at the Assyrian court at Nineveh.

A Biblical passage describes how an Israelite king 'and all the people danced with all their might' in holy rejoicing. In the Jerusalem Temple, groups of singers accompanied by lutes and harps chanted lines in turn and the clash of cymbals punctuated their rhythms. In Israelite tradition music-makers were held in such esteem that the Book of Genesis ranks their calling with that of metalworkers and the owners of flocks. The Assyrian king Sennacherib was evidently delighted with the 'male and female musicians' he exacted in tribute from King Hezekiah of Judah, and boasted about them.

After the fall of Jerusalem, the exiles sitting 'by the waters of Babylon' sang so hauntingly of how they remembered Zion – Jerusalem – that 2500 years later the Biblical lyric provided the basis for a modern popular song. The melodies are lost forever, but it is clear that the Israelites had their familiar favourites. Psalm 22, for instance, was to be sung to a tune called 'The Hind of the Dawn'.

TOYS, GAMES AND GAMBLING

Children enjoyed making lots of noise with toy whistles and rattles and mimicked grown-ups by playing 'pretend' games like 'weddings' and 'funerals' – in other words, childhood pastimes then were much as they are now. The prophet Zechariah could imagine nothing more idyllic than 'the streets of the city full of boys and girls playing'. They had spinning tops and toy animals that could be tugged along with a cord and they played a kind of hopscotch as well as a combination of marbles and skittles.

Youths practised archery with bull's-eye targets much like those of today, and shepherds whiled away their vigils by honing their skills with the sling. Team sports and athletic endeavour for its own sake were Greek concepts, part of a cultural revolution that swept through the waning Old Testament world of the 3rd century BC with an impact comparable to that of American culture on the modern world. But wrestling contests under organised sets of rules went all the way back to pre-Biblical times, and the temptation to race chariots was as irresistible as wagering on the result.

Gambling was so widespread that it was presumed also to be a weakness of the gods. As well as betting on chariot races and the like, gamblers played games of chance using dice and small counters. Some early dice were two-sided discs, others four-sided pyramids, but today's six-sided dice were already in use by the 16th century BC.

Like the exquisite lyres found in the royal tombs of Ur, board games had achieved sophistication well before the time of Abraham. The popularity of a kind

TIMBREL PLAYER The tambourine-like timbrel was used to set the rhythm in singing and dancing.

of ludo played on a board with 20 squares spread from southern Mesopotamia to the Nile. Boards of the rich were beautifully crafted and had interior drawers to hold the pieces. Other games in which counters moved according to the throw of the dice took many forms. In one Egyptian variant, sets of ivory pegs in the shape of dogs and jackals raced each other around a palm tree.

The annual holiday was quite unknown except in the sense understood by those monarchs who beat the bounds of their empires once a year to gather tribute and indulge in some big-game hunting. Holidays were holy days and their number grew with time as the benefits of civilisation afforded – among the elite of the cities at least – increased opportunity for reflection and relaxation.

Bringing In The New Year

Each state's year was punctuated by major seasonal festivals that were religious in context but social in expression. Merchants and entertainers homed upon these occasions to create the first fairs.

For splendour nothing could compare with the New Year festival of the Babylonians and Assyrians, which might best be defined as a Christmas, Halloween and Mardi Gras rolled into one. This spring rite lasted 11 days and included spectacular processions and chanted mime plays

GAMING WITH BOARDS Archaeologists have unearthed a wealth of board games (above) and the pieces and dice (right) used to play them. Games played included a kind of draughts, ludo, solitaire and chess.

JOYS OF DANCE Dancing women beat the rhythm on hand drums in this Egyptian relief. On the right the men have their arms upraised in more angular movements.

in which the gods overcame the forces of chaos and renewed the mandate of the king for another year.

Excitement built up at the approach to Nisan – the month of the spring equinox when the festival took place – as the best craftsmen worked on precious idols to be used in the coming rituals and foreign princes and other dignitaries began to arrive. The first four days of Nisan were taken up by purification rituals and sacred incantations behind temple walls.

On the fifth day, crowds that had assembled on the streets took to lamentation and wailing, with the more histrionic among them dashing about in distracted abandon, for it was understood that Babylon's supreme god Marduk had been spirited off to the nether world leaving the city unprotected. Tension mounted on the sixth day with the arrival of the images of gods from other cities, including Marduk's son and saviour Nabu. The crowds thronged the river banks to catch glimpses of the idols being off-loaded from sacred barges as the king poured welcoming libations.

Next day brought reassurance when the golden image of Marduk was displayed in the ziggurat, his reign restored once more. On the eighth day a solemn, anticipatory hush fell over the city while in templed seclusion the king and priesthood paid attendance upon a conclave of the gods: all the idols were arranged in proper order before that of Marduk, to whom they dedicated their powers.

The ninth day – Nisan 9 – was the day the population had been waiting for. In grand procession, the idols led by Marduk and his goddess consort Ishtar, some in chariots, others borne high on pallets, accompanied by the king and his guests and trailed by a mighty throng, left the inner city for the Festival Temple in a beautiful garden setting beyond the walls. Dazzled by the sight of the images and feeling heady from the billowing clouds of incense and the tuneful trill of the flutes, the mob roared its approval as the king addressed their national deity: 'The Lord of Babylon goes forth – the lands kneel before him.'

At the garden shrine, tableaux depicting the creation of heaven and earth were enacted and the gods' conquest of primordial chaos celebrated with a royal banquet. Mass revelry greeted the returning procession on the following day and that night the marriage of god and goddess was enacted by the king and a priestess. The formal ceremonies concluded with a second convocation of the gods at which humankind's destiny was secured for a further year. The 12th day saw the departure of guests and visiting idols. The satiated public, nursing hangovers, returned to their daily round.

THE PLEASURES OF PILGRIMAGE
The religious feasts of the early Israelites were virtually family picnics, with wine to wash down the lamb stew, and singing and dancing to round out the day. When religion became focused on the

---

REJOICE . . . BUT NOT TOO MUCH
The inclusion of the sensuous Song of Songs in the Biblical canon is credited to the persuasive powers of a venerable rabbi named Akiva in about AD 100. Tradition has it that he added a proviso: 'He who, for the sake of entertainment, sings the song as though it was a profane song, will have no place in the next world.'

HUNTING IN THE PARKS OF PARADISE

HUNTING was the sport of kings, second only to warfare in the case of the Assyrian monarchs who, while on campaign, enjoyed combining their two favourite pursuits.

The organised hunt originated as a sacred royal duty to control the numbers of dangerous beasts like lions and bears and the herds of gazelles and wild asses that took a toll on crops. In time, with the depletion of wildlife, game parks were created and stocked.

Tiglath-pileser I of Assyria set a gruelling tempo in the late 12th century BC. Lions were still a scourge in his day and a few wild elephants lingered in parts of northern Syria. On one of his 28 expeditions against the Aramaeans, he bagged 920 lions and four elephants, according to scribal records. He also tried his hand at game fishing in the Mediterranean and harpooned a 'nahiru', probably a whale or dolphin.

The Syrian lion, a small sub-species, was headed for extinction under the onslaught from royal hunters, and kings took to augmenting wild prey with captive breeding programmes and by importing African lions. The beasts were released from cages in a park to be pursued in chariots and disabled by arrows, then speared or finished with a sword-thrust.

Lions were not the only animals consigned to royal safari parks. The Assyrian monarchs accumulated substantial zoological collections of gazelles, deer, leopards, bears, elephants and the now-extinct wild ox which the public were permitted to view. The kings also collected rare botanical species for their parks.

By the 5th century BC the Persians were mounting still grander hunts. A hunting park in the Aramaic language was *prdys* and in Persian it was *paridaisa*, from whence comes our word 'paradise'.

HUNTING THE LION   Reliefs from Nineveh show King Ashurbanipal, an enthusiastic sportsman, in pursuit of lions.

SPRING HARVEST A procession of country people makes its way to a local sanctuary to celebrate the barley harvest.

Jerusalem Temple, pilgrimages to the city became the custom. Before their Babylonian exile, they had three great annual festivals. The first was partly rooted in pre-Biblical spring rites – a lambing celebration of nomadic origin and another that marked the gathering of the spring barley crop. Gradually combined, this became a commemoration of the Israelites' deliverance from Egyptian bondage: the feast of the Passover.

Each family killed a male lamb and smeared some of its blood on their door-posts. Then they roasted the carcass and feasted upon it through the night. Simple barley bread without yeast ('unleavened') was eaten with the meal and for the next seven days. Seven weeks later, the Feast of Weeks ushered in the wheat harvest, when the heads of farming families cut the first sheaves and with

other 'first-fruits' delivered these as offerings to the Temple priests.

The Feast of Ingathering, or simply 'The Feast', was a bacchanalian celebration of the wine and olive harvests that originally took place in the groves and vineyards. Transferred to the city, the tradition was maintained by families camping out in gardens or on the roof of their homes in little brushwood huts.

This was the major celebration of the Israelite year, when everyone let themselves go – the prophets speak of joy, gladness and 'shouting'. Once focused upon the Temple in the capital, it assumed the character of a New Year festival in which the king sought divine assurance for the coming seed-time and the next agricultural cycle, and the people joined in a torchlight procession.

MIND, BODY AND SPIRIT

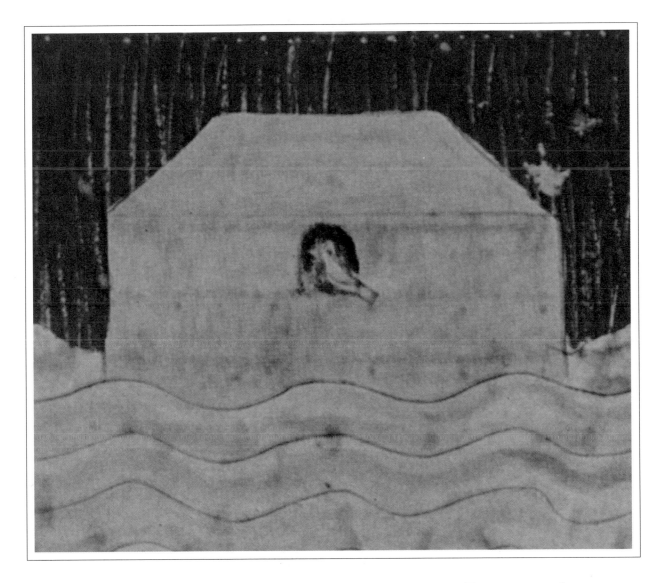

Tales of a universal deluge were told among many Near Eastern peoples –
surviving in the Biblical story of Noah's Ark (depicted in a medieval
manuscript above). Most peoples worshipped many gods; the Israelites were
remarkable in developing the worship of a single, unseen God, to become
one of the most potent influences in all human history. The healing arts,
meanwhile, drew on religious beliefs as well as traditions of folk medicine.

FABULOUS TALES OF CREATION

Near Eastern creation stories shared many features, notably the emergence of the world from the waters of primeval chaos. Aspects of the Biblical narrative, such as Eve's creation from Adam's rib, can be traced back to the much earlier Sumerian accounts.

THE BIBLE'S stately opening words would have found ready recognition among most Near Eastern peoples of Abraham's time in the 18th century BC and for at least 1000 years before that: 'In the beginning God created the heaven and the earth. And the earth was without form, and void; and darkness was upon the face of the deep. And the Spirit of God moved upon the face of the waters.'

Generation upon generation of priests, poets and minstrels had passed down wondrous tales of how life began – tales lacking perhaps the exceptional, distilled splendour of the Book of Genesis, but anticipating many of

**AND GOD SAID . . .
'Let the earth put
forth vegetation' –
from a medieval
Jewish manuscript.**

its principal images. The capacity to memorise is very highly developed in preliterate societies, and the lyre-strumming minstrel or *nar*, in particular, was a living, performing archive. His large repertoire was eventually set down after – often a long time after – the first development of writing. A fraction of this rich lore survives to this day, retrieved from the royal libraries of the Assyrians and from tablets dug from Babylonian ruins.

CONTESTS WITH CHAOS

Both the Egyptians and the Mesopotamians conceived of everything emerging out of a watery chaos. Out of the waters, so the early Egyptians imagined, a hill arose and squatting upon it was the sun god who set about creating the universe. 'O Atum-Kheprer [the sun god], thou wast on high on the primeval hill,' runs a dedication text from a 24th-century BC pyramid. 'Thou didst spit out what was Shu [the god of air], thou didst sputter out what was Tefnut [goddess of moisture].' This was a reflection of the fertile hillocks that emerged each year as the life-giving flood waters of the Nile subsided.

CONCEPTS OF THE UNIVERSE

AMONG THE peoples of the ancient Near East, the cosmos was commonly seen as a watery chaos within which the heavens and the earth were enclosed in the manner of an upturned goldfish bowl.

Above the earth and anchored upon mountain pillars at its extremities was a dome sometimes thought to be made of tin. This sealed in the sun, moon and stars and held back

the waters of chaos, except on those occasions when a deluge was unleashed through the agency of divine wrath.

Beneath the earth was the abyss, the Great Deep of subterranean waters (the Biblical Tehom) which welled up as springs and rivers. Uncomfortably situated below ground in close proximity to the abyss was the gloomy abode of the dead.

This is the vision reflected in the Second Commandment's reference to 'heaven above . . . the earth beneath [and] the water under the earth'. Psalm 104 puts it poetically in describing how the Lord 'layeth the beams of his chambers in the waters' and covered 'the foundations of the earth . . . with the deep as with a garment' so that 'the waters stood above the mountains'.

LET THERE BE LIGHT Illuminations in a 14th-century Hebrew manuscript represent different stages of the creation.

To the Mesopotamians of the Euphrates and Tigris flood plain, the cause of creation seemed self-evident from the manner in which life teemed from the reed beds where river and sea met and mingled. From this observation and from the treacherously bountiful nature of their environment with its twin threats of flood and drought, people fashioned a theology depicting a cosmic struggle between order and chaos.

By Biblical times, this was being expressed in a creation epic that was chanted during the New Year festivals in the Babylonian and Assyrian capitals. The starring role was alternatively ascribed to the two peoples' national gods, Marduk and Ashur, but in substance the epic harked far back to the concepts and gods of the vanished Sumerians of the 3rd millennium BC.

Known as *Enuma Elish* ('When on high') from its opening line, the epic tells how in the beginning nothing whatsoever existed but the primordial forces of fresh and salt water, Apsu and 'Mother' Tiamat. In a mingled mating Apsu and Tiamat produced a boisterous brood of divine beings who became overbearing and rebellious:

> *When on high the heaven had not been named,*
> *Firm ground below had not been called by name,*
> *Naught but primordial Apsu, their begetter,*
> *And Mummu-Tiamat, she who bore them all,*
> *Their waters commingling as a single body;*
> *No reed hut had been matted, no marsh land had*
> *appeared,*
> *When no gods whatever had been brought into being,*
> *Uncalled by name, their destinies undetermined –*
> *Then it was that the gods were formed within them.*

When one of these deities, the god Ea, subjugated Apsu, the distraught Tiamat created another squad of divinities to help to fight her offspring. In the Babylonian version, the offspring made the young Lord Marduk, son of Ea, their champion.

QUEEN OF HEAVEN

Ishtar, the supreme goddess of Babylon, manifested herself in many forms including the Greek Artemis, whose temple at Ephesus in modern Turkey was one of the Seven Wonders of the ancient world. Eastern traditions assert that Mary, mother of Christ, found her final earthly refuge in Ephesus and it was here, in 431 BC, that the Christian church officially approved the title 'Mother of God' (*Theotokos*) for Mary.

Marduk armed himself with a bow and mace, lightning, the four winds and a net. Then, mouthing a spell, he mounted his storm chariot drawn by the four steeds Killer, Relentless, Trampler and Swift. He enraged Tiamat – who had taken the form of a giant sea serpent – by challenging her to single combat and was on the point of being consumed when he whipped up a mighty wind. This rushed into Tiamat's belly, forcing her mouth wide open. Into the yawning jaws he fired an arrow, ripping the serpent's insides and slitting her heart.

As his enemies cowered in abject surrender Marduk split up the corpse of Tiamat 'like a shellfish' and with one half he created the canopy of heaven and with the other the dry land, parting and holding back the waters of chaos in the process. He set up stations for his fellow gods in the heavens and the gods, by mingling clay with the blood of the commander of Tiamat's forces, created humankind – whose job was to serve them.

NOAHS BEFORE NOAH

For the people of Biblical times, humanity's relationship with the gods, as with the elements, was far from secure and the return of chaos was an ever-present threat. Stories of a divinely brought deluge date back to Sumerian times. In the earliest known version, a pious king named Ziusura is tipped off about the gods' intentions to destroy 'the seed of mankind'. He is able to save himself and all life forms by building a huge boat in which to weather out the ensuing flood until the sun god comes to the rescue with his drying rays.

In a later Babylonian version, the gods decided to bring the flood because humanity was becoming too rowdy. Again one man was warned in advance, this time by the god Ea, and he proceeded to build a mighty ark with six decks into which he packed his family, his craftsmen and 'the beasts and wild creatures of the field'.

ELEMENTAL SCENE Nightfall brings out strange colours in the Judaean landscape. The fertility of such lands depended on rains sent, it was believed, by a bountiful god.

FLOOD FRAGMENT The story of the Flood as told in the Mesopotamian Epic of Gilgamesh is given in this tablet.

The deluge was so great that even the gods crouched in fear. 'All light was turned into darkness . . . the water climbed over the mountains', recounted Utnapishtam, the Babylonian 'Noah'. When the storm abated, he opened a window in the ark and wept to find that 'all was sea'. Eventually a mountain peak emerged from the receding waters.

Utnapishtam released a dove, which found nowhere to perch and so returned. Then he released a swallow, which also returned. Finally he released a raven which 'croaked and came not back'. Utnapishtam then freed his cargo and on top of the mountain he prepared so savoury a sacrifice that the mollified gods 'crowded around like flies'.

The Biblical account ends with a sacrifice, too, and with a promise from Yahweh never again to inflict such disorder: 'Then Noah built an altar to the Lord, . . . and offered burnt offerings on the altar. And when the Lord smelled the pleasing odour, the Lord said in his heart, "I will never again curse the ground because of man, . . . ; neither will I ever again destroy every living creature as I have done. While the earth remains, seedtime and harvest, cold and heat, summer and winter, day and night, shall not cease".'

The theme of combat with a primordial chaos-monster likewise passed from people to people. The gods of the highland Hittites to the north slew dragons in their myths, while the Canaanites and Phoenicians had a myth cycle in which the storm god Baal-Hadad fought Yam, 'Prince Sea', who sometimes took the form of a seven-headed sea serpent.

The seasonal crises of winter flood and summer drought were the focus of many poetic myths involving the temporary disappearance or death of a deity. This happened to both the fertility goddess *continued on page 130*

GILGAMESH – HE WHO SAW EVERYTHING

Near Eastern peoples of the 2nd and 1st millennia BC thrilled to
the adventures of Gilgamesh, history's first recorded superhero.

GILGAMESH was a real person whose exploits passed into myth in the same manner as the legends of King Arthur. After centuries of embellishment, the stories were crafted into an epic saga by a Babylonian scholar-priest. It is the earliest recorded work of literature, and addresses the great themes of friendship, loyalty, humanity's high aspirations and tragic fate.

'He who saw everything' – so the story begins – was a tall, strong, handsome prince of Uruk (Biblical Erech) whose mother was a minor goddess in service to the sun god Shamash. This made Gilgamesh part god, yet also mortal. Fearless and wilful, he outraged everybody by chasing married women and banging the sacred kettledrum just for fun. To put him in his place, the gods created a hairy wild man named Enkidu, as strong as Gilgamesh himself.

Gilgamesh set out to tame Enkidu using a temple seductress who 'was not bashful as she welcomed [Enkidu's] ardour . . . for six days and seven nights he possessed her ripeness'. After that, Enkidu was a changed man. He was rejected by his friends the wild beasts, and so docile that his lover could lead him about hand in hand.

Having robed, oiled and domesticated her wild man, the girl took him to the city where he confronted Gilgamesh. They wrestled like wild bulls, shattering gateposts and making the walls shake, until Gilgamesh realised he had met his match and the pair embraced.

Gilgamesh and Enkidu became boon companions in the adventures that followed. These included an expedition to the Forest of Lebanon where they slew its fire-breathing giant and felled some of the famous cedars. The love goddess Inana-

DELIVERING THE MORTAL BLOW
Enkidu holds onto the Bull of
Heaven, allowing Gilgamesh to
strike home with his sword.

Ishtar was impressed enough to offer herself to Gilgamesh, but he knew that her love spelt death for mortals. He spurned her.

The rejected goddess let loose the Bull of Heaven, a monster whose hot breath was the desert wind and who could slay hundreds with one snort. Again the partners triumphed, Enkidu grappling with the bull until Gilgamesh was able to kill it with a sword thrust.

They returned home in triumph, but Ishtar cursed Enkidu with a disease which led to his death. Bereft, Gilgamesh set out in quest of the meaning of life. He wore the skins of lions and lived off their flesh as he wandered plains and scorching deserts until he came to the rim of the world. Here a twin-peaked mountain holding up the roof of heaven was guarded by scorpion-men with glowing halos.

The scorpion-men admired his courage and let him enter a tunnel under the mountain. He groped his way through the darkness for many miles until he emerged in a garden of jewelled fruits that glittered dazzlingly in the sunlight.

From here he followed the sun's path to the Waters of Death, which by great daring and with the help of its ferryman he managed to cross. On the far side he was met by Utnapishtam, the Mesopotamian Noah, who had been granted eternal life for his service in the Great Flood, but who advised him that immortality was not only impossible to attain, but boring.

Gilgamesh was given a magic plant enabling him to stay young and strong. But it was stolen by a serpent who demonstrated its powers by shedding its old skin.

Gilgamesh journeyed home, wiser and with a new sense of pride in his city's stout-walled splendour and in mortal accomplishment. The moral of the epic was delivered in a few lines of advice: 'So, Gilgamesh, accept your fate. Wash, bathe and don fresh clothes. Eat well, dance, sing and play. Make each day and night a celebration. Enjoy your wife and cherish the little child who clings to your hand. For this is the task of mankind.'

TEMPTATION AND THE FALL
The serpent is wrapped
around the 'tree of the
knowledge of good and
evil' in this medieval
Sicilian mosaic. It depicts
Adam and Eve being tempted
in the Garden of Eden.

Apart from such obvious and well-known examples as the Flood and the primordial waters of creation, the Biblical holy Mount Zion harks back to Zaphon, a mountain retreat of Baal, and even the curious tradition of Eve's creation from Adam's rib can be traced to a 3rd-millennium BC poetic myth concerning the paradise of the Sumerians.

This delectable garden of the gods, much like the Biblical Eden, contained certain plants sacred to the Mother Goddess. When the god Ea was tempted into eating the plants he became cursed with rib and other injuries. To help to cure the wounded Ea, a healing deity named Ninti was created. Ninti means 'the Lady of the Rib', but it can also be translated as 'the Lady who Makes Life', because in Sumerian hieroglyphs the sign for 'rib' and 'life' is the same. By Biblical times, the significance of this literary pun had been lost, but the connection endured – and endures – in the Genesis story of Eve's creation.

Inana-Ishtar and her lover Dumuzi, god of sprouting vegetation. In one fabulous tale involving a cast of fierce deities, the goddess suffered excruciating indignities at the hands of her sister and foe, a goddess of death. Inana-Ishtar only secured her release from the underworld by nominating her lover as substitute. The tale concluded with a compromise whereby Dumuzi was committed to spend half the year in the underworld and his sister, a goddess of the grape harvest, the other half.

TROUBLE IN PARADISE

The Israelites inherited this trove of myth, some of which is woven into Genesis and is alluded to throughout the Bible in vivid imagery and many obscure references now clarified by scholars.

A HISTORY OF THE CROSS

Millennia before Christians adopted the cross as their symbol it was a symbol of Shamash, the Mesopotamian sun god (from whence the Biblical hero Samson's name derives, as does the Arabic word for the sun, *shams*). To the Egyptians the cross symbolised the productive force of nature. It was the monogram of the god Osiris and was also worn on the vestments of priests of Horus.

GODS, PRIESTS AND PROPHETS

Different gods were identified with different natural phenomena – from the sun to the

wind to thunder. Among the monotheistic Israelites, reforming prophets brought

new emphasis to religion, including a concern for social justice.

NAMING GOD This 6th-century BC amulet is the earliest-known instance where the name 'Yahweh' is written down.

OLD TESTAMENT MINDS seethed with thoughts, hopes and fears of the supernatural. No single word for religion existed (the Hebrew 'fear of God' is the nearest) because religion – in the widest sense of humanity's relationship with the unseen – was not just one aspect of people's lives, but their very basis. Through ritual, omen and divination, the powers of good and evil were constantly being watched, consulted and propitiated through offering and sacrifice.

From pre-Biblical times, each culture had inherited a complex pantheon of gods and goddesses who were believed to control its destiny and who might be coaxed, bribed and begged into improving its lot and averting disaster. These pantheons had probably evolved out of worship of the elements upon which survival depended.

A GATHERING OF GODS

While all natural phenomena were thought to be imbued with an invisible spirit, different cultures emphasised different ones depending on local conditions. Thus the peoples of Mesopotamia and Egypt, living by great rivers upon which they relied for many necessities, believed water to be the supreme creative – and destructive – force. It was abetted by the sun and in Mesopotamia by the hot,

flood-drying wind. Desert nomads concentrated on the wheeling wonder of sun, moon and stars.

The heavenly hosts multiplied to meet individual needs, with a god dedicated to each activity, from motherhood to brick-making. The assiduous scribes of Sumer in the early 2nd millennium BC listed 3600 deities. Then, as peoples met and mingled, so did their gods whose names and attributes became increasingly entangled.

MANY IDOLS Most Near Eastern cultures had a multitude of gods dedicated to particular activities.

There was order, however, within the confusion for the gods assumed family based hierarchies. Each pantheon had as its supreme deity a lofty, remote patriarch who ruled over an extended family of squabbling siblings with goddess-wives and children. Each city or tribe revered some member of the pantheon as its own protective deity, and with the growth of city-states and then empires, a few deities gained stature far beyond their original status.

By the 1st millennium BC the most powerful national gods – reflecting the political and military might of the peoples who worshipped them – were Ashur of the Assyrians and Marduk of Babylon. Baal, which meant 'lord', 'master' or even 'devourer', was the epithet for various closely related gods presiding over Phoenician and Aramaean city-states.

Capturing the popular imagination throughout the Near East was the goddess known as Ishtar to

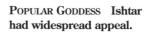

POPULAR GODDESS   Ishtar had widespread appeal.

the Mesopotamians and as Astarte to the Canaanites. In assorted guises, she was revered as a sympathetic intermediary with the major gods. She was also the ultimate femme fatale, a vibrant goddess of love and fertility as well as of war, dubbed both 'lady of heaven' and 'lady of sorrows and battles'. The Israelites, coming from desert nomad stock, originally envisaged their god Yahweh as a thunder god bearing lightning bolts and making the earth tremble.

IDOLS ON THE MARCH

For most Near Eastern peoples, images of the gods and goddesses exerted power in their own right. Armies marched behind them and traders took small copies on their travels as powerful talismans. Enemy temples were not only plundered for their riches, but for the psychological value of captured idols. Uniquely in the Near East, the Israelites made no images of Yahweh, but the mobile shrine of their early days, the Ark, was credited with supernatural powers of protection and destruction, fatal to touch or to peer into.

Large and powerful priesthoods staffed a state god's temple, which was the preserve of royalty and the seat of national pride. No expense was spared in its construction and improvement as each king sought to outshine the last. 'I covered its walls with sparkling gold,' Nebuchadnezzar of Babylon reported of the shrine to Marduk. 'I caused it to shine like the sun.' Here, wrote the Greek historian Herodotus, was 'the great sitting figure of Marduk all of gold, on a golden throne supported on a base of gold with a golden table standing beside it'. Outside was a golden altar.

As national treasuries, temples became prime targets for invaders.

THE HOLY ARK   A relief from a Jewish synagogue at Capernaum in Galilee gives a depiction of the Ark of the Covenant from New Testament times. Right: An engraving from the 16th century AD shows the Ark being carried around Jericho.

THE POWER IN A MAGIC NUMBER

MYSTICAL POWERS were widely attributed to certain numbers which had great symbolic significance, though in some cases the reasons for this are buried beyond recall in prehistory.

SEVEN represented the sum of the heavenly bodies that had been

SEVEN IN MESOPOTAMIA
Winged figures marked out the buildings protected from evil by the seven sages (*apkallu*).

individually identified and tracked since earliest times – the Sun, the Moon and the five planets Mercury, Venus, Mars, Jupiter and Saturn. It was invested with peculiar potency and features often in Mesopotamian and Biblical allusion and ritual, sometimes as its multiple **FOURTEEN**. Its hold endures in the seven-day week and in references like the seven deadly sins, seven days of creation, seven ages of man, seven wonders of the world, seven seas, seventh heaven and the seven hills of Rome and numerous other cities. . . .

FORTY signified fullness, being the multiple of ten and **FOUR**, from the 'four corners of the earth'. It was the measure of many Biblical events. The Deluge lasted 40 days, the tribes under Moses spent 40 years in the wilderness – as Jesus would later spend 40 days being tempted there – and both David and Solomon reigned for 40 years. Its importance survives in our word quarantine, which meant 40 days.

SIXTY was sacred to the Sumerian god Anu. It was the basic unit of mathematical calculation in conjunction with **TEN**, the tally of fingers and thumbs and source of the decimal system. The importance of 60 endures today in our 60 minute hour and 360 degrees of the circle. French retains an echo of the ancient system of calculation with its word for 70, *soixante-dix*, which translates as 'sixty and ten'.

Physiologists suspect that there is a biological basis to some of these number fixations. They point to seven's association with the natural rhythms of nature, from the spin of the sun – at a fraction short of seven days – to the waxing and waning of the moon through four quarters of seven days and the human menstrual cycle that matches this lunar month.

Under a Biblical injunction in Leviticus, a woman was enjoined to wait seven days after her period and then to offer a sacrifice of purification. Whether intentionally or subconsciously, the priestly regulators were focusing upon the point in the monthly cycle when conception was most likely.

Solomon's Temple in Jerusalem was sacked several times before its final destruction in 587 BC by the Babylonians. Yet such was the extent of its assets that hundreds of sacred vessels were said to have survived the Babylonian pillage to be returned with the repatriated Judaeans two generations later.

While priesthoods toiled to propitiate the gods through sacrifice, seers sought to consult them through omens and prophecy. Many techniques were used at different periods, until the craft achieved its most sophisticated level among the Babylonians, whose centuries of celestial studies led to the birth of astrology as well as astronomy. An early and enduringly popular approach was to examine the liver of a sacrificed sheep; the slightest variation from the normal carried a message for the trained interpreter, who had a clay 'standard' model for comparative purposes.

Dream interpretation was a specialisation of women. Other diviners interpreted the gods' will through the shapes assumed by drops of consecrated oil in a bowl of water, or the drift of smoke from a censer. Among the Israelites, sacred dice were used to take decisions – a process known as 'casting lots' – with the result credited to divine guidance.

Movements of the moon, sun and stars, and phenomena such as earthquakes or severe storms were considered particularly prophetic in matters of statecraft. Royal watchers scoured the skies for portents that were interpreted from tablets compiled over centuries of observation. 'If the sun

stands above or below the moon, the throne will be secure', Babylonians believed. But: 'When the moon and sun are seen together on the sixth day of the month, war will be declared on the king.'

Ecstatic prophecy was an old Canaanite tradition. Prophetic individuals and bands typically worked themselves into frenzied trances with dancing and music, sometimes even cutting themselves with knives, and in that state they uttered their oracles: in one Biblical episode, 450 prophets of Baal and 400 prophets of Asherah (Astarte) worked themselves into a frenzy of this kind, only to be confounded by a solitary miracle-working prophet of Yahweh, the great Elijah.

RUSTIC ALTAR TO THE ROYAL TEMPLE

Ordinary people were largely excluded from worship in royal temples. Most had to be content with what they could glimpse from afar, or in the course of sacred processions. Each individual also had a personal god who acted as a kind of guardian angel; local and household shrines existed to cater to the needs of such deities.

Early in the Israelites' history their tribal elders conducted rustic rituals at 'high places' – *bamoth* – dotted about the hills. These open-air sanctuaries, often on sites hallowed from time immemorial, consisted of a stone platform on which sacrifices of animals and of produce such as oils and fruit were offered. This form of religion was later replaced by a centrally focused state worship of Yahweh overseen by an hereditary priesthood.

The Israelites' later temples were an adaptation of a Canaanite design. The earliest Israelite temple so far discovered by archaeologists dates from about 1000 BC – the approximate time of King David – and

HIGH PLACE An Israelite tribal elder offers a libation at a hilltop *bamoth* ('high place').

FEASTS WORTHY OF THE GODS

COMPLEX RITUAL and liturgy attended every aspect of state worship, which was based upon a daily round of offerings punctuated by purification ceremonies and grand seasonal festivals. As basic a job as putting a new skin on one of the big temple kettledrums of Babylonia and Assyria was an excruciatingly complicated procedure involving many days of precisely prescribed priestly activity.

Temple worship was focused upon the god-images, often made of precious woods and richly adorned. In a Mesopotamian temple, the effigy of a great god was treated as a divine king, attended by the effigies of minor and servant-gods and by vigilant priest-courtiers and a large temple staff. The effect was like that of a modern child caring for its doll's house, only on a grand and solemn scale. Each effigy had a wardrobe of clothes which were changed according to the sacred calendar. Meals were served at least twice daily behind closed curtains to the accompaniment of sacred music and incantations. When the gods had 'eaten', their hands were ritually washed. Much more food was prepared than could be placed before the gods and in this way the temple and royal establishment might be fed.

Lesser states supported humbler establishments, but the concept of security through sacrifice was rooted in every people's tradition. To ensure the fertility of their herds and lands, the early Israelites made offerings of goats, sheep and a portion of their crops at high places or on family altars. This evolved into elaborate sacrificial rituals focused upon the Jerusalem Temple, where the altar had to be enlarged to cope with so much slaughter. Procedures involving the sprinkling of blood alternated with offerings of wine and grain soaked with olive oil that had been brought to extra purity in the temple precincts.

A small offering of flour, or one or two pigeons, was sufficient contribution from the poor, but anyone of consequence was expected to present livestock to be slaughtered by the priests as *zevach* or *olah* – peace offerings or burnt offerings.

With *zevach*, the intestinal fat was burnt on the altar and the meat cooked for the worshippers. With *olah*, the entire carcass was burned to a cinder; only the hide was saved as the priests' portion. Clouds of costly frankincense helped to cloak the stench of burning fat. For the Temple's rededication under King Hezekiah shortly before 700 BC, the Bible states that 70 bulls, 1000 rams and 200 lambs went up in smoke, while a further 3600 beasts were slaughtered as peace offerings.

A KING'S OFFERING   Ashurbanipal of Assyria pours a libation over four dead lions as an offering to the gods.

ASSYRIA'S GOD
Ashur is shown in stylised form with a drawn bow.

served the people of Arad, an Israelite stronghold near the southern end of the Dead Sea. A courtyard with sacrificial altar led into a small chamber, with low benches for offerings set around the walls. Incense tables flanked a tiny inner chamber in which stood a smooth stone pillar.

The Arad temple was closed around 715 BC when the reforming King of Judah, Hezekiah, strove to centralise worship in Jerusalem. Anything remotely resembling an idol, including the simple monoliths of stone or wood that had long been popular, was proscribed, but people found it hard to adhere to the austere demands of the unseen Yahweh. Inscriptions left about this time by merchants at a small Israelite shrine on a trade route through the Sinai demonstrate the diversity of popular belief. Here invocations to Yahweh, Asherah and Baal were juxtaposed with images of the Egyptian dwarf god Bes.

ORTHODOXY AND BACKSLIDING

The Hebrew Bible measures kings of Israel and Judah by the strength of their devotion to Yahweh, but the Biblical record also demonstrates how difficult such orthodoxy was to enforce. Priests themselves did not always draw a line in their conduct between devotional zeal and drunken debauchery, and the Book of Isaiah describes them stumbling about with 'all the tables full of vomit'.

The split between Judah and Israel compounded the problem.

Cut off from the Temple in Jerusalem, worship of Yahweh in the northern kingdom was controlled by its rival monarchy and developed differences: in place of the Temple's winged angelic Cherubim, for instance, the north had a golden calf as a sacred guardian beast. For reasons of expediency or through political pressure, even the Jerusalem Temple was not always kept sacred to Yahweh alone – as the prophets frequently complained. Affording other peoples' deities guest facilities was a Near Eastern tradition and even so notable, if pragmatic, a figure as King Solomon raised shrines to the gods of Moab and Ammon, while including Asherah (Astarte) in court worship.

Astarte continued to enjoy at least sporadic royal patronage and the favour of ordinary Israelite folk as a time-honoured deity of motherhood and fertility. Small terracotta images of the goddess were mass-produced for hundreds of years, sometimes brightly painted and rouged, and a cache of more than 350 figurines found in a cave within 100 yd (90 m) of the Temple Mount in Jerusalem may date from the crackdown by King Josiah in 621 BC. According to the Biblical record, this was when the high priest Hilkiah was ordered to throw out of the temple and destroy all cult objects 'made for Baal and for Asherah [Astarte] and for all the [heathen] host of heaven'.

SUN GOD
Shamash sits facing a sun disc, his emblem.

'O SOLE GOD, LIKE WHOM THERE IS NO OTHER!'

AS EARLY AS the 14th century BC the aesthetic, iconoclastic Egyptian pharaoh Amenhotep IV pioneered a form of monotheism by proclaiming Aton, the sun disc, the one universal god.

Amenhotep renamed himself Akhenaton, 'spirit of Aton', and decreed a sophisticated minimalist faith focused upon veneration of the prime source of light and life. In one startling move after another, he tried to cast aside the clutter of anthropomorphic Egyptian gods, their secret rites and the death cult of mummification.

Following his death, the priesthood had its vengeance. The pharaoh was damned as a heretic and all was as before, yet his 'Hymn to the Sun Disc' made such an enduring impression that some of its imagery – praising the god who ordered the universe in all its richness and diversity – was used by the Biblical psalmists writing many centuries later:

All beasts are content with their
pasturage;
Trees and plants are flourishing.
The birds which fly from their nests,
Their wings are stretched out in
praise of thy ka [vital force].
All beasts spring upon their feet.
Whatever flies and alights,
They live when thou hast risen
for them.
The ships are sailing north and south
as well,
For every way is open at thy
appearance.
The fish in the river dart before thy face;

Thy rays are in the midst of the great
green sea....

How manifold it is, what thou hast
made!
They are hidden from the face of man.
O sole god, like whom there is no other!
Thou didst create the world according
to thy desire,
Whilst thou were alone:
All men, cattle, and wild beasts,
Whatever is on earth, going upon
its feet,
And what is on high, flying with its
wings.

The countries of Syria and Nubia,
the land of Egypt,
Thou settest every man in his place,
Thou suppliest their necessities:
Everyone has his food, and his time of
life is reckoned.

Psalm 104 sings Yahweh's praises in remarkably similar terms:

Thou makest springs gush forth in
the valleys;
they flow between the hills,
they give drink to every beast of the field;
the wild asses quench their thirst.
By them the birds of the air have their
habitation;
they sing among the branches.
From thy lofty abode thou waterest the
mountains;
the earth is satisfied with the fruit of
thy work.

Thou dost cause the grass to grow for
the cattle,
and plants for man to cultivate,
that he may bring forth food from the
earth,
and wine to gladden the heart of man,

oil to make his face shine,
and bread to strengthen man's
heart....

O Lord, how manifold are thy works!
In wisdom hast thou made them all;
the earth is full of thy creatures.
Yonder is the sea, great and wide,
which teems with things innumerable,
living things both small and great.
There go the ships,
and Leviathon which thou didst form
to sport in it.

These all look to thee,
to give them their food
in due season.
When thou givest to
them, they gather
it up;
when thou openest
thy hand,
they are filled with
good things.

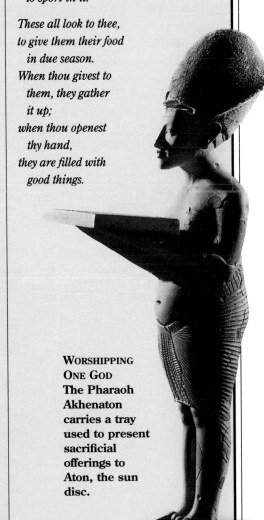

WORSHIPPING ONE GOD The Pharaoh Akhenaton carries a tray used to present sacrificial offerings to Aton, the sun disc.

LIFE-GIVING RIVER 'Hark, the roar of the lions, for the jungle of the Jordan is laid waste!' The Biblical prophets, such as Zechariah here, make several references to the thick, lush vegetation along the banks of the Jordan.

No amount of religious purging could bring about a lasting effect. Samaria, the capital of Israel, had already fallen to the Assyrians in the century before Josiah, and under the terms of a peace settlement Josiah's predecessor King Ahaz of Judah had been obliged to commission and erect an altar to the Assyrian god Ashur. Succeeding kings were rarely able to avert alien intrusion.

Judah and Jerusalem survived Josiah's reign by barely two decades and these years saw a gaudy diversity of cult practices, from temple worship of the Assyrian-Babylonian sun god Shamash to 'weeping for Tammuz', a rite in which seeds were sprouted and then allowed to die to the accompaniment of lamenting for a god whose annual death marked the summer drought.

SOCIAL ORDER AND RIGHTEOUS LIVING

The Near Eastern ideal of righteous living had always involved obedience to the social order, to elder brother and older sister, to parents, to master, on up the hierarchy through the ruler to the minor and great gods. Sins included not only obvious wrongdoing and violations of social norms, but transgressions against innumerable sacred taboos, such as eating a food or straying into an area proscribed by a particular deity, even if in all innocence.

The gods were final arbiters and the most that a pious and just person could hope from them was a long and fulfilling lifetime, since people had no expectations of resurrection or heavenly reward. The dead – always provided they received decent burial – were consigned willy-nilly to a subterranean 'land of no return'. This place was known as Kur to the Mesopotamians and Sheol to the Israelites, who viewed it with gloomy finality. 'The dead praise not the Lord', laments the Biblical psalmist, who in one instance uses this idea in a deathbed plea to Yahweh: 'Oh save me for thy mercy's sake. For in the grave there is no remembrance of thee; in the grave who shall give thee thanks?'

On the other hand, there were also people who questioned abject surrender to the fates and sought a profounder meaning to existence. By exploring the problem of undeserved suffering, the 500 line Babylonian 'Poem of the Righteous Sufferer' anticipated the Biblical Book of Job. The poetic sufferer contrasted his exemplary conduct with his many afflictions and concluded that divine purpose was beyond human comprehension.

> *If I only knew what found favour with the gods.*
> *What is good in one's own sight is evil to a god.*
> *What seems bad pleases the god.*
> *Who can understand the gods in heaven?*

In 14th-century BC Egypt Pharaoh Akhenaton tried to impose the worship of the universal god Aton, the sun disc. Elsewhere, through a process of conquest and assimilation, increasingly potent gods arose to provide something more substantial in the form of a supreme and sometimes merciful deity, like Marduk, 'whose gentle heart sustains the dying'. By the 7th century BC the Babylonians were being enjoined to act with a magnanimity that foreshadows the Sermon on the Mount:

> *Do not do evil unto your enemy; answer evil with*
> *good . . .*
> *Clothe and honour the beggar so that his god rejoices.*

This begged the question that intellectuals were asking themselves. It has been preserved in the form of an elegantly written dialogue in which a disillusioned sufferer and his pious friend debate human misery and oppression. The sufferer is unimpressed by his friend's constant reassurances:

> *They who do not seek the god go the way of prosperity.*
> *They who pray to the goddess fall into poverty and*
> *weakness.*
> *From my youth I sought the will of the god;*
> *With abasement and prayer I followed my goddess.*
> *It was all a pointless chore,*
> *For the god gave me poverty instead of riches.*
> *A cripple gets ahead of me, a fool is in front of me;*
> *The rogue is promoted; I am laid low.*

The Babylonians had no answer for this, but in Judah and Israel a radical new breed of activist emerged and redefined the meaning of the word prophet. Mostly aristocrats with royal connections, they were impassioned individualists who raged against the uglier aspects of material progress, such as corruption and land-grabbing by the rich – 'grinding the faces of the poor', they called it.

Starting with Amos during the 8th century BC, they denounced 'false prophets' of the popular

continued on page 142

THE TEMPLE OF SOLOMON

Nothing survives of Solomon's Temple, but the Biblical record supported by archaeological evidence from Phoenician temples makes a reconstruction possible. It appears that the Israelites glamorised it in their memories, since the temple was not outwardly imposing. It was a box with a ground plan of 120 by 40ft (36 by 12m).

Its glories lay within – the walls panelled with cedar sheathed with gold and ornamented with carvings of winged creatures, palm trees, flowers and buds, all overlaid with gold. Light from apertures under the eaves pierced the incense-laden gloom to define dimly the curtained inner sanctuary. This was the Holy of Holies containing the Ark of the Covenant beneath the wings of a pair of carved beasts, the Cherubim. It was here that the Shekinah, or divine radiance of Yahweh, dwelt.

PURIFYING FLAMES Zoroastrian believers kept a sacred fire permanently alight on this altar in Persia.

miracle-worker kind and the fertility-obsessed cult of blood sacrifice. Over the course of 150 years they scolded and coaxed kings such as Hezekiah and Josiah into enacting their reforms.

Speaking through the likes of Micah and Isaiah, Yahweh emerged as an ethical god disgusted by the rigmarole of traditional ritual: 'To what purpose is the multitude of your sacrifices to me? Bring no more vain oblations; incense is an abomination unto me . . . your new moons and your appointed feasts my soul hateth.' Man's only responsibility was 'to do justly, and to love mercy'.

The prophets could not, however, save Israel or Judah from the consequences of evil, and some modern economists even argue that the reforms they instigated fatally weakened both states by causing severe unrest and stifling enterprise. But they set the tone for the culture and faith that would develop in the aftermath of the Babylonian exile and influence future civilisations to the present day.

Extraordinary changes in mental attitudes were also taking place elsewhere in the Near East and beyond it, spurred by thinkers who looked away from the deities of nature and tribe towards more spiritual or universal explanations of existence. When the prophet Jeremiah was growing up in Judah in the late 7th century BC, for instance, the Greek philosopher Thales of Miletus was expounding the revolutionary theory that the gods were not responsible for such phenomena as earthquakes and lightning – that instead natural explanations had to be sought through scientific investigation.

HEAVEN, HELL AND SATAN

When in 539 BC the conquering Persians rolled into Babylon they brought the people of the Bible new theories of religion and morality as well as freedom. The Persian monarchs embraced the theology of a visionary named Zoroaster, who had died little more than ten years before their conquest of Babylon. He preached against magic, idolatry and animal sacrifice and denounced the old polytheistic gods as evil demons. In their place he exalted Ahura-Mazda, the Wise Lord, all-seeing creator of heaven and earth and champion of truth and light, and he turned traditional Persian fire worship into a purification ritual.

Zoroaster gave new meaning to human existence by offering a novel solution to the philosophic dilemma of evil. He portrayed the universe as a battleground between truth and light and the powers of darkness and falsehood led by Ahura-Mazda's implacable adversary Ahriman, demonic champion of 'the lie'. All individuals were personally embroiled in the mighty struggle between good and evil and how they conducted themselves in life would determine their fate when at the end of time the forces of darkness were defeated. On that day of reckoning the virtuous would be granted heavenly salvation; the rest consigned to everlasting fire.

In Babylon the priests and scribes defining Judaism came into contact with Zoroastrianism, as the faith became known, and it made a profound impression on them. In turn it would influence the theology of both Christianity and Islam. All would embrace the concept of heaven and hell, while the evil spirit Ahriman is still with us, as Satan.

CURSE, CURE AND QUACKERY

The Egyptians had specialist medical men from before 2000 BC. By 1000 BC

the Babylonians and the Assyrians had two kinds of medical practitioner:

asus, who were physician-pharmacists, and *ashipus*, who were priest-exorcists.

NOTHING EARNED the gods so much wary respect as the fear of illness. Injuries were explicable, but disease was hard to fathom other than by reference to the supernatural, and so medical treatment evolved as a combination of faith healing and folk medicine. By the 5th century BC an information-exchange on remedies was flourishing in the public market in Babylon, according to the Greek historian Herodotus.

Egyptian mummies are medical time capsules. Opened up, they reveal lives beset by chronic aches and pains that run the gamut from tuberculosis, polio and smallpox to ulcers, gallstones, varicose veins, appendicitis, hernia, hardened arteries and piles. Virtually every mummy examined has a worm infestation and sometimes several, often including bilharzia (schistosomiasis), the waterborne parasitical disease that plagues much of Africa today.

FLOWER POWER Women press flowers to extract a juice they will use to make perfumes and medicinal oils. Oils and special resins – such as the Biblical balm of Gilead – were applied to cleansed wounds.

SPIRITUAL PROTECTION **The words inscribed on this bowl were believed to protect its user from evil spirits.**

The situation differed little across the Near East. Dusty, insanitary conditions fostered eye disease. Arthritis was common as were chronic lung complaints caused by inhaling sand particles and the smoke from fires and oil lamps in poorly ventilated homes. Flies, polluted water and primitive hygiene facilitated the spread of epidemics, which in turn encouraged belief in collective punishment. 'Let us put disease in the land with mankind', one god says to another in an early Mesopotamian myth.

'COME, REMEDY, COME . . . '

Fevers, like mental disorders, were easily ascribed to possession by demonic figures such as Lamashtu, the pestilential she-devil of the Babylonians and Assyrians. To counterbalance her were more benign spirits like 'the Seven and Seven' that might be enjoined to intervene through incantations. Practical approaches were not ignored and from pre-Biblical times patients were being rubbed, poulticed and dosed to sometimes positive effect with compounds made from plant and mineral extracts.

The Egyptians were the first to specialise. Before 2000 BC they had eye, bowel, head and even enema specialists; they also had nursing auxiliaries called 'bandagers'. Spells enhanced fanciful prescriptions that were intended to root out malignant entities. 'Come, remedy, come, you who expel evil things from my belly and limbs!' began one incantation to be recited while drinking a potion that might include dung, urine, fly dirt or other noxious ingredients designed to disgust the demons into vacating their victim. Religious scruples against tampering with corpses held up the development of scientific anatomy, even if the Egyptians benefited from the practical experience of mummification. By the 2nd millennium BC, however, the importance of the heart was realised, if not its precise function. Egyptian doctors felt a patient's pulse, which they tried to interpret as a 'voice'.

A surgeon's manual from 1700 BC, incorporating knowledge acquired much earlier, indicates that the pyramid-builders were able to cope with some of the injuries associated with heavy construction work. Fractured collarbones and broken limbs were set as well as possible and held with linen-bound splints. Burns were treated with greasy substances and lint was used as surgical dressing.

THE GP IN 1000 BC

The Babylonians and Assyrians developed two medical disciplines, one operating through sacred magic, the other attempting to cure by relatively practical means. The *asu* was a physician-pharmacist and the *ashipu* was a priest-exorcist. They might

STRUCK DOWN BY THE GODS

The term 'stroke' in reference to a cerebral haemorrhage is a modern reflection of ancient belief in the power of a god to strike down anyone who incurred his wrath. The expression 'moonstruck' similarly reflects ancient belief in the moon's divine powers to cause epilepsy.

SCAPEGOATS AND HOW TO EXORCISE DEMONS

BABYLONIAN SHE-DEMON
A fearsome lion-headed demon brandishes a snake in each hand and has a pig and a dog hanging from her breasts.

Set up a tripod of cedarwood over the image and surround it with a circle of flour. At sunset, place over the tripod an inverted pot in which nothing has been cooked. Burn incense of juniper resin and each night heap up offerings of finest flour before the stars.

Keep repeating the prescribed incantation. After three days and nights seal the mouth of the pot and bury it in deserted wasteland.

The notion of trapping an evil entity inside a pot is reflected in the Bible, in the Book of Zechariah, which instances a figure representing wickedness being confined in a lead container. The Hittites similarly believed that evil spirits were confined in the nether world in bronze cauldrons with lead lids.

INCENSE BURNER
Burning incense was part of the rituals sometimes used to exorcise demons. This incense stand was found at Megiddo.

DEMONS AND GHOSTS victimised the virtuous and wicked alike and were considered a prime cause of illness. Fortunately, they were as stupid as they were spiteful and could sometimes be tricked into vacating their victim through a simple ploy, such as having the sick man share his bed with a kid goat. The idea was to confuse the evil spirit into entering the goat, at which point the goat's throat was slit.

This theory of substitute sacrifice became part of Babylonian and Assyrian religion when, as part of the New Year festival, a sheep loaded with the people's sins was cast into the river with due ceremony. The scapegoat abandoned to the wilderness by the Israelites sprang from the same tradition.

Chronic cases of possession demanded all the expertise that the Mesopotamian priest-magician could muster. The exorcism procedure used by the Assyrians was prescribed for ailments ranging from arthritis to dizziness and mind disorders. It required the co-operation of the sun god Shamash, whose help was petitioned by means of a lengthy spell recited in conjunction with these instructions:

Take dirt from ruined buildings, a ruined temple, a grave, a neglected garden, an abandoned canal, a disused road; mix in bull's blood and make of it an image of the evil thing.

Clothe the image in lionskin and a necklace of carnelian and make it grasp a leather bag containing provisions. Stand it on the roof of the sick man's house. Pour a libation.

HEALING POWERS   An Assyrian seal shows a male patient, lying down, being ministered to by priestly healers.

work together as a team, and though magic was widely trusted, the asu was sufficiently effective for Babylonians to have a saying that 'illness without a physician is like hunger without food'.

The asu was a general practitioner par excellence, master of a pharmacopoeia of substances that he mixed, pounded, cooked or boiled into medicines, ointments and vaporous stews. It included items such as belladonna (deadly nightshade), a notorious poison when not diluted. Narcotics like opium and hashish, or more often alcohol, gave some relief when he wielded his bronze lancet. Posted to military duty, the asu was adept at patching up arrow and other basic wounds.

The ashipu, meanwhile, attributed ills to a god, demon or ghost and treated patients with magical prescriptions once he had divined the supernatural agent. For this he had only to consult his tablets. Archaeologists have even unearthed 'delete-where-inapplicable' charts for general use that anticipates modern computer diagnostic techniques:

— son of —, whose god is —, whose goddess is —, who is sick/dying/distraught/ troubled, who has eaten food taboo to his god [goddess]/has lied/crossed his god [goddess]/oppressed a weak woman/caused a family row/despised his parents/offended his elder sister/had sex with his neighbour's wife/shed his neighbour's blood/slept in the bed/drank from the cup/sat in the chair of a person under a curse . . .

. . . and so on. The problem was duly identified by elimination and the ashipu prescribed accordingly.

Sympathetic magic sometimes played a part in such prescriptions. The earliest known treatment for baldness was a potion whose 'active' ingredient was hedgehog quills, while an attempted cure for blindness involved the use of a pig's eye. The ashipu was also alert to signs and portents. If he happened to see a black pig, that could be interpreted as a bad omen, whereas spotting a white pig was usually regarded as a good omen; seeing a corpse pointed to a full recovery.

GARLIC SNIFFING AND PREGNANCY TESTS

Pregnancy and the perils of childbirth were pressing concerns. The Babylonians devised a pregnancy test, which involved the insertion of a tampon impregnated with plant juices. This acted like litmus, changing colour according to the acidity of the patient's secretions. It certainly represented an improvement on urine-sniffing and other such customs, including the vaginal insertion of garlic: if the patient breathed garlic next day, it was reasoned that she had no internal blockage.

CHILDBEARER
Women might employ midwives who offered magical as well as practical skills.

WEAR AND TEAR Surgeons treated the injuries of construction workers such as these slaves in an Assyrian quarry.

Word of a particular doctor's success spread far and wide. Egyptian and latterly Greek physicians were in vogue with princes who had the power to summon the best available talent. For all the hocus-pocus, there was a sophisticated realisation of the limits to expectations – at least among the elite. In the 13th century BC a Hittite king asked the Egyptian pharaoh Ramses II to send a doctor with drugs to help his sister conceive. 'Look, my brother, I know your sister and she is 50, if not 60,' the pharaoh wrote back. 'What you request is impossible. But just put the matter in the hands of the sun god and the weather god [the senior Hittite gods] and whatever they determine will surely come to pass.' The pharaoh sent a doctor all the same, and 'an able magician' as well.

In their anxiety for a safe delivery, the well-to-do consulted diviners. One spell invoking the moon god called for the woman in labour to be sprayed with water and rubbed with oil containing bits of broken pots, so that 'her waters do not remain, as water does not in a broken vessel . . .' In the case of a difficult birth, the woman was required to fast and drink beer infused with herbs.

DIAGNOSING BIBLICAL AILMENTS

MODERN DIAGNOSIS has been brought to bear on the illnesses that beset Biblical people. Some plagues and ailments are easy enough to identify, but others defy analysis.

Sennacherib lifted an Assyrian siege of Jerusalem when an epidemic struck down his army, according to the Second Book of Kings. Since the Biblical account makes no mention of any of the defenders being affected, medical sleuths rule out the possibility of a contagious plague. They suggest that Sennacherib's troops might have contracted malaria on their march from the north and that chilly nights camped out in the Judaean hills brought on fatal attacks – which is what befell a contingent of British troops sent to Jerusalem to recuperate from malaria during the Second World War.

One of the most perplexing of Bible stories concerns Isaac's son Esau, who traded his inheritance with his younger brother Jacob in return for a bowl of 'pottage', or

COUGH CURE This 5th-century BC tablet from Nineveh gives details of how to treat a cough.

lentil broth. Esau has usually been characterised as a stupid glutton, but an intriguing medical solution has been proposed.

The Book of Genesis relates that Esau was feeling faint and 'at the point to die' after a day spent out of doors when he accepted his younger brother's hard bargain.

According to Genesis, Esau was also remarkable for being unusually husky and hairy. He could have suffered from hypoglycaemia, or low blood sugar, as a complication of a congenital condition in which the adrenal gland produces an excess of hormones that upset the balance of body sugars and fats.

This causes rapid muscular and hair development during childhood, but it makes victims subject to sudden, dangerous collapse if they ever overexercise. The high-protein broth and the barley bread that went with it would have provided the delirious Esau with a quick corrective.

Some doctors consider another story, of how Elisha revived a dead child, to be proof that mouth-to-mouth resuscitation was practised in the 9th century BC. 'And he went up, and lay upon the child, and put his mouth upon his mouth,' II Kings relates. 'And the flesh of the child waxed warm . . . and the child sneezed seven times, and the child opened his eyes.'

People's frustration in the face of the limitations of medicine is most evident from the Hebrew Bible, which cites only one prescription – a fig poultice applied to a bothersome boil on King Hezekiah of Judah. It tends to favour a direct resort to divine intervention, criticising King Asa of Judah for having a doctor treat his gout instead of relying upon Yahweh, in whose name Deuteronomy sternly declares: 'I kill, and I make alive; I wound, and I heal.'

Cries of helpless suffering are to be found in the Psalms. 'My God, my God, why hast thou forsaken me?' Psalm 22 begins. 'Why art thou so far from helping me?' What follows, when rendered into modern colloquial English, is a telling description of a delirious fever: 'I am weak as water and all my bones are out of joint. My heart has sunk into my bowels. I have no more strength than a broken pot and my voice is a bone-dry death rattle . . . I can count my bones: . . .'

PROPHETIC HEALING

A desperately sick Israelite could make offerings, or seek out a holy man in the tradition of Elisha, the healer-prophet who lived through six reigns and was credited with several miraculous cures. The other recourse was to herbal remedies, some still familiar, but many now lost or obscure (among which the 'balm of Gilead' enjoyed a particularly high reputation). Vinegar was regarded as a cure-all, drunk to lessen fatigue and applied to wounds and bruises. Other standbys included sycamore figs, mustard seed, the balsam shrub, aloes for burns and pulverised hyssop leaf for skin sores.

At one point the prophet Isaiah likened Judah to a bruised and battered person and in so doing gave a glimpse of how wounds were treated: 'From the sole of your foot to the top of your head there is no soundness – only wounds and bruises and open sores, not cleansed or bandaged or soothed with oil.' Soothing ointments were made from sheep fat and olive oil and to ease pain there was gall, a soporific drug extracted from the opium poppy and mixed with wine, vinegar and myrrh.

The observation in Ecclesiastes that 'dead flies cause the ointment of the apothecary to send forth a stinking savour' suggests an awareness of the dangers of dirt. The Israelites also demonstrated a keen sense of the preventive and cleansing properties of running water.

Israelite priests doubled as public health inspectors, inasmuch as they oversaw laws governing communal health and personal hygiene and a dietary code whose arcane regulations reflected, at least in part, a wisdom born of practical experience. Their rituals called for frequent hand-washing, while the rite of circumcision was believed to help to prevent venereal disease. Other regulations helped to contain contagion through isolation and primitive attempts at disinfection.

On the evidence of the Bible, leprosy – probably a mixed diagnosis of several chronic skin conditions – was a particular scourge. Priests monitored skin eruptions or other telltale signs every seven days to see whether the condition cleared up. If it did not, the cry of 'unclean, unclean' was raised. The afflicted person's clothes were burned and he or she was declared defiled and banished from inhabited areas; finally, the vacated home was scrubbed down with a wash containing powdered hyssop leaves. Not even kings were excused under such circumstances. When Uzziah (Amaziah) of Judah contracted a skin disease in about 750 BC he was obliged to appoint his son regent and live out his days in isolation.

CLEAN-OUT **The home of a diagnosed leper is cleansed with a disinfectant solution made using hyssop leaves.**

149

TIME CHART

INNOVATION
A Hittite chariot with spoked wheels.

THE NEAR EAST

SYMBOL OF POWER **The pyramid of Khufu (right), still one of the largest buildings in the world.**

2500 BC The Great Pyramid at Giza is 50 years old.

2300 BC Humble-born Sargon of Akkad ends Sumerian hegemony and unites Mesopotamia to create the first empire. Sea trade between the Euphrates and the Indus Valley in present-day Pakistan is at its height.

2100 BC Stepped temples – ziggurats – begin to dot the Mesopotamian plain.

1900 BC Normal weather patterns resume after a prolonged drought, bringing in its wake social disruption and nomad incursions.

1850 BC The spoked wheel, introduced from the Asian steppes by the Hittites, spurs development of the chariot; the Hittites also introduce horse-racing.

1792-1750 BC The deft and energetic Hammurabi of Babylon reunifies Mesopotamia. His major legacy is an exhaustive legal code reflecting a mix of Sumerian justice and harsh desert custom.

1730-1570 BC The Hyksos, alien pharaohs coming from beyond the Sinai desert, rule Lower Egypt. They are said to have introduced the horse and chariot to Egypt.

1700 BC A jar of cloves from about this date, unearthed in Syria, is evidence of a 5000 mile (8000 km) trade link with the East Indies.

THE CANAANITES AND HEBREWS

2500 BC The area of present-day Israel is dotted with independent petty kingdoms, each with its well-fortified town. The total population is about 150 000.

1900 BC From the mountains of Asia Minor and around Mesopotamia, restless, bothersome mercenary bands collectively known as 'Hapiru' – possibly meaning 'dust-raisers' – operate across borders in Canaan.

1880 BC A family band of 37 'sand-crossers' – tinkers with flock, bellows and anvil – from Shutu (the Biblical Sheth) is painted on an Egyptian tomb. It is the only contemporary depiction of a patriarchal-type clan known to exist.

NOMADS A group of Semitic traders on their way to Egypt.

ZIGGURAT **This stepped temple is among the remains at Ur.**

1750 BC The saga of the Biblical Patriarchs, as told in Genesis, begins with the journey of Abraham's family from Ur in southern Mesopotamia.

THE REST OF THE WORLD

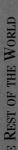

PADDY FIELDS Farmers plant out rice seedlings in irrigated fields.

2500 BC Skis are in use in Scandinavia; soon the hardy northerners will ease their lives by inventing the sauna.

2200 BC Extinction of the mammoth is complete when the last small herd dies out on the Rangel Island off the Siberian coast.

2000 BC Cultivation of rice in flooded paddy fields to increase yield is established in South-east Asia.

1900 BC Minoan civilisation on Crete approaches its exuberant zenith. The airy, multicoloured palaces are brightly decorated with frescoes and have bathrooms with running water. The origins of bull-fighting can be traced to Minoan acrobatics performed with a charging beast.

1876 BC The first precisely datable event in history happens on October 16: a solar eclipse recorded by astronomers alarms the court of Zhong Kong in northern China.

1800 BC Collapse of Harappan civilisation in the Indus Valley. It is due in part to incursions of mounted Aryan nomads, equipped with bronze weapons, from across the Hindu Kush.

1750 BC The Shang dynasty replaces the Xia rulers in China. The Shang kings, regarded as semidivine by their subjects, establish a state centred on the Yellow River plain.

GIFT-BEARERS From a fresco at the Palace of Knossos, Crete.

POTTERY CHARIOT Terracotta figures from the Indus Valley.

1500 – 1201 BC

SUN WORSHIP Akhenaton and Nefertiti give praise to the sun god Aton, on a temple relief.

1500 BC The *shaduf*, a water bucket attached to a weighted pole, is introduced in Egypt and greatly reduces the toil of raising water from irrigation canals and depositing it on crops. The device is still in use today.

1450 BC A massive volcanic eruption destroys the Greek island of Thera and impacts upon nearby Crete, which within 50 years is

CONQUERER Ramses II with prisoners, on a limestone stele.

conquered by Mycenaeans from mainland Greece.

1430 BC In a consignment of tribute Pharaoh Tutmosis III receives a gift of 'birds that lay eggs each day';

the chicken, long domesticated in the Far East, makes its debut.

1356 BC Pharaoh Akhenaton incurs priestly wrath by trying to enforce worship of a single deity manifested by the life-giving sun.

Nefertiti was Akhenaton's wife. Her name means: 'The Beautiful One is Come.'

1285 BC Clash of empires: Ramses II's Egyptian army and the Hittites battle to a stalemate at Kadesh in Syria.

1250 BC Mycenaean Greeks attack Troy in an early phase of warfare that erupts around the eastern Mediterranean, destroying the Hittite Empire and many small states.

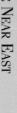

1441 BC Pharaoh Amenophis II lists 3600 'Hapiru' among his war captives. Subsequent Egyptian texts refer to Hapiru captives being employed as

WAR LEADER Amenophis II ruled Egypt at the height of its military power.

servants and stone-hauliers, just as the Biblical 'Children of Israel' were required to do.

1360 BC Hapiru raiders harry a number of Canaanite principalities including Jerusalem.

1224 BC Pharaoh Ramses II dies. Biblical scholars usually reckon that the Exodus of the Israelite people led by Moses happened during his reign.

1220 BC Pharaoh Merenptah claims the destruction of 'Israel' – the first and only reference to Israelites in Egyptian records.

DESTRUCTION The Israelites are defeated in Canaan by the forces of the pharaoh Merenptah.

1500 BC Canoe voyagers reach Samoa and Tonga from New Guinea about this date to complete the first phase of Pacific settlement.

1500 BC Chinese craftsmen use ceramic moulds to mass produce bronze vessels.

1500 BC Composition of the Vedas (books of knowledge) begins in India. So does the caste system, springing from the race-consciousness of the fair-skinned Aryan conquerors.

1490 BC Hunters in Nevada fish with multihook lines and lure wildfowl with duck decoys identical to their modern counterparts.

EARRING Egyptian jewellery was traded far and wide.

1475 BC Amber from the Baltic is being traded around the Mediterranean and Egyptian beads are reaching England and Ireland.

1440 BC The final version of Stonehenge is complete on the Wiltshire Downs in England.

1400 BC Cultivation of the drought and flood-resistant soya bean, native to Manchuria, spreads through China. With its by-products oil, sauce and bean curd it becomes a dietary staple, invaluable in times of famine.

TEMPLE OR OBSERVATORY? Built in three phases over 1300 years, Stonehenge's purpose is unknown.

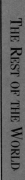

1200 – 901 BC

THE NEAR EAST

VICTORS Egyptians lead off captive Philistines, from a temple relief.

1180 BC The Sea Peoples, a loose, aggressive alliance of Aegean and Mediterranean folk, overthrow the Hittites but are repulsed at the Nile delta by Egyptian land and naval forces. Some groups scatter to settle elsewhere. The Peleset (Philistines) stop in their tracks to settle along the coast.

1190 BC Egypt, depleted by war and trade dislocation, suffers a rash of royal tomb robberies.

1100 BC The Assyrians develop the use of massed heavy infantry as a counter to the chariot. Indefatigable Tiglath-pileser I fights his way to the Mediterranean and by his death in 1077 BC has mounted 28 campaigns against the Aramaeans.

1100 BC A few weapons of carburised and quenched iron – steel – are being produced in the Near East.

975 BC The Phoenicians begin to exploit the trading void with ambitious merchant voyages and improvements to ship designs.

950 BC Iron tools are coming into general use, ushering developments in farming, construction and manufacturing.

METAL TRADE An incense burner shows a Phoenician copper trader.

THE ISRAELITES

GREAT KING **David brings the Ark to Jerusalem, in a medieval Bible.**

1100 BC Under local commanders (the Judges) the Israelites struggle to fend off the Philistines and are pinned down in hilly back-country, which they cultivate by conserving winter rainfall in water-tight cisterns.

1020 BC The warrior Saul is appointed commander-in-chief with royal powers. His end comes some 20 years later when he commits suicide after his forces have been overwhelmed by the Philistines.

1000 BC About this date David captures Jerusalem from the Jebusite clan and proceeds to forge a thriving kingdom with a string of victories. By 975 BC he has eliminated the Philistines as a major threat.

961 BC Solomon succeeds his father David and embarks upon an ambitious development programme, including an expansion of the capital, Jerusalem.

931 BC Political schism following the death of King Solomon causes division into the rival kingdoms of Israel and Judah.

924 BC Jerusalem's royal palace and Temple are sacked by Pharaoh Shosenq (Shishak) I .

BUILDING WORKS A 19th-century interpretation of the Temple of Solomon.

THE REST OF THE WORLD

JAGUAR SPIRIT **An Olmec jade figurine of an animal spirit.**

1200 BC Olmec civilisation, the mother culture of Central America, emerges on Mexico's Gulf Coast. Without the benefit of the wheel, iron tools or draught animals, 20 ton sculptures are carved and brought from distant mountains and complex water systems are created over the next 600 years. Olmec deities, temples and designs will influence future cultures, including the Mayan and Aztec.

1200 BC Farmers begin to terrace steep slopes of the Andes to increase crop production and fight erosion.

1100 BC The Zhou dynasty succeeds the Shang by conquest and expands China's 'Middle Kingdom' from the Yellow River to the Yangtze.

1050 BC Celtic culture is born on the upper Danube. Oats are also domesticated in central Europe about this time.

950 BC Incessant civil warfare inspires creation of the *Mahabharata*, India's national epic. At 100 000 couplets it is the longest poem known.

CHARIOT FIGHT A 16th-century illustration from the *Mahabharata*.

BUFFALO A bronze figurine from the Zhou dynasty in China.

ASSYRIAN ATTACK A carved relief shows Tiglath-pileser III leading an assault on the city of Upa.

745 BC Brilliant, relentless Tiglath-pileser III presses a policy of permanent conquest consolidated by mass deportations that within a dozen years advances Assyrian power to the borders of Egypt.

713 BC Sargon II of Assyria fortifies a square mile with palaces, temples, armouries and noble dwellings at Khorsabad. On Sargon's death, his just-completed project is abandoned when his successor Sennacherib builds Nineveh.

680 BC The aqueduct, conceived in the mountains of Armenia, is adopted by the Assyrians. It will play a major role in urban development.

MASTER BUILDER Sargon II is depicted with a nobleman.

THE KING IN NINEVEH Sennacherib rides out in his chariot.

671 BC Esarhaddon of Assyria marches on Egypt and takes Memphis to unite the Fertile Crescent under one rule for the first time.

612 BC Nineveh falls to a force of Medes and Chaldeans, ushering the collapse of the Assyrian Empire and restoration of Babylon as the seat of Middle Eastern power.

605 BC Nebuchadnezzar II crushes Pharaoh Necho's expeditionary force at Carchemish to clinch Babylonian domination of the Near East.

THE NEAR EAST

HOMAGE Jehu, King of Israel, brings tribute to Shalmaneser III.

868 BC Completion of Samaria, Israel's custom-built capital. The royal palace is notable for its fine ivory fittings.

853 BC At the Battle of Qarqar in Syria, a 12 nation force including 14 000 Israelites manages to halt an Assyrian advance.

841 BC A woman, Athaliah, rules Judah after a year of bloody coups in which the kings of Israel and Judah and their families are butchered. Athaliah is executed six years later.

Jehu of Israel bows before Shalmaneser III and pays off Assyria with tribute.

745 BC Prosperity turns to turmoil under redoubled Assyrian pressure. Israel has five kings inside ten years.

722 BC Samaria is destroyed after a three-year siege. After deportations, Israel becomes the Assyrian province of Samaria.

705 BC Judah suffers near disaster when King Hezekiah backs a revolt crushed by Sennacherib of Assyria.

640-609 BC King Josiah tries to bolster Judah and curb alien influence through social and religious reforms.

UNDER SIEGE The Assyrians besiege Lachish in Judah.

ISRAEL AND JUDAH

NEW TOWN Carthage was a major sea power in Classical times.

814 BC Phoenicians found Carthage ('New City') on the North African coast. In the centuries to come it establishes a trading empire.

SPORTING HEROES Wrestling at the Olympic Games.

776 BC The first recorded Olympic Games. The Games are held every four years in honour of the god Zeus and are marked by a cessation of all armed conflicts.

753 BC Traditional date for the founding of Rome.

750 BC Around this date the Greeks adopt and adapt the Phoenician alphabet.

720 BC In central Italy, the Etruscans are making false teeth of bone with gold bridges.

700 BC The *Iliad* and *Odyssey*, epic poems based upon the Trojan War, are composed and credited to the blind Greek poet, Homer.

EPIC EVENT Achilles kills Hector, as described in Homer's *Iliad*.

THE REST OF THE WORLD

600 – 301 BC

THE NEAR EAST

NEW MONEY
A coin, minted on the orders of King Croesus.

600 BC About this date, a Phoenician crew circumnavigates the continent of Africa.

550 BC Croesus, King of Lydia, mints the first gold and silver coins.

539 BC Cyrus the Great conquers Babylon for Persia.

522-486 BC Darius I completes the expansion of the Persian Empire, which reaches from India to Greece and is spanned by highways and a Nile canal linking the Mediterranean and the Red Sea.

MOSAIC   Darius III of Persia at the Battle of Issus.

404 BC The exploits of the Ten Thousand (actually 13 000) fighting as mercenaries under Xenophon in a Persian civil war stir the Greek world.

333 BC Alexander the Great defeats Darius III of Persia at the Battle of Issus. The Persian king flees the field, leaving behind his wife, mother and children.

331 BC Alexander the Great takes Babylon and then carries his campaign as far as Kashmir. He completes the obliteration of the Persian Empire, bringing Greek culture to the fore.

323 BC Alexander the Great dies at Babylon after a reign of just over 12 years.

FACE OF POWER
A portrait head of Alexander the Great.

THE JUDAEANS AND THE JEWS

597 BC Nebuchadnezzar takes Jerusalem and deports the royal household, a portion of the aristocracy and the best crafts people to Babylon.

LEARNED MEN
Scribes were teachers and legal experts.

587 BC Jerusalem is sacked, its walls torn down and the Temple levelled after an abortive revolt.

582 BC Destruction of Jerusalem is completed, with more deportations, after the Babylonian-appointed governor and his staff are assassinated.

570 BC Scribes work on the early books of the Bible. The table of nations in Genesis 10 is assembled about this time.

538 BC Following the Persian conquest of Babylon, the exiled Israelite community is given the option of returning home, but most are unenthusiastic.

520 BC Persia appoints a member of the royal family in exile to govern renamed Judaea, thus encouraging more families to return.

516 BC The rebuilt Temple is dedicated in Jerusalem.

440 BC Through the efforts of the priestly scribe Ezra and others, Judaism is established as a codified religion.

THE REST OF THE WORLD

THE BUDDHA
Gautama Siddhartha.

563 BC Birth in the Himalayan foothills of Gautama Siddhartha, founder of Buddhism.

551 BC Birth of Confucius, whose philosophy of dutiful obligation will dominate Chinese attitudes.

509 BC Roman patricians abolish the monarchy and establish a republic.

490 BC Athenians repulse a Persian invasion at Marathon. The Persian threat is ended following further land and sea battles in 480 BC.

438 BC Completion of the Parthenon, Athens.

410 BC The Greek philosopher Democritus postulates that all matter is composed of invisible particles in constant motion – atoms.

399 BC Socrates, aged 70, is sentenced to death and takes poison.

390 BC A Celtic horde from beyond the Alps sacks Rome. The citizens buy it off with gold and start to rebuild.

GREEK SAGE   Socrates' influence dominated Greek philosophy.

MEETING OF MINDS
Confucius and Lao-tzu, founder of Taoism, in an 18th-century painting.

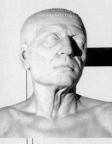

ROMAN ORATOR Cicero opposed Julius Caesar's undermining of the Roman republic.

250 BC The invention around this time of valves, gears and the leaf spring spur a spate of experimentation and such innovations as a water pump and an improved catapult. Ctesibius of Alexandria demonstrates steam power, but puts it to no practical use.

193 BC Introduction of concrete, made from rubble, volcanic ash and lime, revolutionises Roman construction techniques. Because the mix hardens under water,

it facilitates an ambitious harbour-building programme around the Mediterranean.

150 BC Wine production benefits from the development of a screw press to crush the grapes.

63 BC Marcus Tullius Tiro, a freed slave, uses shorthand to

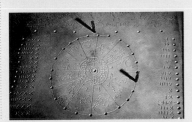

record the speeches of Roman orator and defender of the republican cause, Cicero.

54 BC First Roman invasion of Britain under Julius Caesar.

46 BC The Julian calendar of three 365 day years followed by a leap year of 366 days is adopted, doing away with lunar reckoning. To align the calendar to the seasons, the year 46 BC is accorded an extra 67 days.

10 BC Cranes are in use on Roman construction sites.

MARKING TIME The Julian calendar, marked out with the months and days.

HIDDEN LIBRARY Many scrolls found in caves around Qumran were stored in jars.

250 BC Earliest fragments of the Dead Sea Scrolls – discovered near Qumran on the Dead Sea – date from about this time.

164 BC Religious nationalists, led by Judas Maccabeus and his four brothers, launch a successful revolt against Greek dominance that restores Jewish independence for a time.

63 BC The Romans conquer Palestine.

45 BC Julius Caesar grants the Jews the privileges of a favoured people, including freedom of worship, exemption from military service and the right to remit an annual temple tax to Jerusalem.

MILITARY GENIUS Julius Caesar laid the foundations of the Roman Empire.

19 BC Herod the Great begins to rebuild the Jerusalem Temple on a grandiose scale.

4 BC In the probable year of Jesus Christ's birth, the world Jewish population is estimated to have swollen to 8 million, with the vast majority living outside Judaea.

MODEL FARM A Han dynasty miniature sheep-pen.

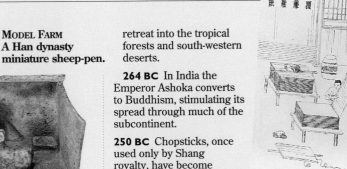

300 BC Ironworking spreads through Nigeria into the rest of sub-Saharan Africa. So do Bantu-speaking cattle herders, displacing resident hunter-gatherer communities who

retreat into the tropical forests and south-western deserts.

264 BC In India the Emperor Ashoka converts to Buddhism, stimulating its spread through much of the subcontinent.

250 BC Chopsticks, once used only by Shang royalty, have become common throughout South-east Asia.

220 BC The Chinese invent gunpowder.

150 BC Polynesian voyagers from Tonga and Samoa reach Tahiti and the Society Islands.

PAPERWORK A Chinese paper-maker makes a press.

130 BC The Chinese make the first paper from hemp and rag waste; it is used as clothing and for toilet purposes.

90 BC Chinese physicians discover the circulation of the blood. About the same time, the Chinese hit upon the first insecticide when they crush chrysanthemums to kill fleas; the active ingredient is pyrethrin.

INDEX

ACKNOWLEDGMENTS

ABBREVIATIONS
T = Top; M = Middle;
B = Bottom; R = Right; L = Left

AAAC = The Ancient Art & Architecture Collection
AKG = Archiv für Kunst und Geschichte, London
BAL = The Bridgeman Art Library, London
TBA = Toucan Books Archive, London

1 Zev Radovan. 2-3 AAAC/Ronald Sheridan. 4 British Museum, London/AKG/Eric Lessing. 5 British Museum, London/E.T. Archive, TL; Zev Radovan, TR, ML, BL; Iraq Museum, Bhagdad/AKG/Eric Lessing, BR. 6-7 Map by Morag Eaton. 8-9 *Bedouin Tents, Jordan*, Christine Osborne. 9 TBA. 12 British Museum, London/BAL. 13 *Landscape of Samaria*/Zev Radovan. 14 British Museum, London/AAAC/Ronald Sheridan. 15 Musée du Louvre, Paris/AKG. 16 AAAC/Ronald Sheridan. 17 Zev Radovan. 18 Zev Radovan, T; Collection Reuben and Edith Hecht, Haifa Universitat/AKG/Eric Lessing, BR. 19 *Olive Grove in Samaria*/Sonia Halliday Photographs. 20-21 *Judean Desert*/AAAC/Ronald Sheridan. 22 *Agricultural Landscape in Judea*/Zev Radovan. 23 Illustration by Paul Wright. 24 Illustration by Gill Tomblin, T; *Village Well in Judea*/Zev Radovan, BL. *Shepherd With Sheep, Israel*/ASAP/Lev Borodulin, T; British Museum, London, B. 26 Musée du Louvre, Paris/AKG/Eric Lessing. 27 *Underground Olive Oil Press, Maresha, Israel*/ASAP/Richard Nowitz. 28-29 Illustration by Sarah Kensington. 30 Roemer und Pelizaeus Museum, Hildesheim/TBA, TR; AAAC/Ronald Sheridan, BL. 31 Musée du Louvre, Paris/AKG/Eric Lessing, T; Illustration by Gill Tomblin. 32 British Museum, London. 33 Zev Radovan. 34 Illustration by Paul Wright. 35 Zev Radovan. 36 Zev Radovan. 37 Illustration by Sarah Kensington. 38-39 Zev Radovan. 40-41 Illustration by Kevin Goold. 42 Zev Radovan. 43 Musée du Louvre, Paris/AKG/Eric Lessing, T; Zev Radovan, MR. 45 BLMJ Borowski Collection/Zev Radovan. 46 Illustration by Gill Tomblin. 47 LIFE Magazine © Time Inc./Photograph by David Lees/Katz Pictures. 48 Zev Radovan. 48-49 Illustration by Peter Morter. 49 British Museum, London/AKG/Eric Lessing 50 British Museum, London/Michael Holford. 51 Aleppo National Museum, Syria/AKG/Eric Lessing, T; British Museum, London/AKG/Eric Lessing, B. 52 BLMJ Borowski Collection/Zev Radovan, TL; Zev Radovan, TM, TR. 53 Illustration by Paul Wright; Israel Museum, Jerusalem/ASAP. 54 Illustration by Christian Hook. 55 British Museum, London/AKG/Eric Lessing, T; ASAP/Richard Nowitz. 56 Zev Radovan. 57 Illustration by Christian Hook, TL; Zev Radovan, BR. 59 Illustration by Sarah Kensington. 60 Zev Radovan. 61 Israel Museum, Jerusalem/ASAP. 62 Illustration by Gill Tomblin. 63 Egyptian Museum, Cairo/Jürgen Liepe, TR; AAAC/Ronald Sheridan, BL. 65 Zev Radovan, T; Illustration by Gill Tomblin, BR. 66 AAAC/Ronald Sheridan. 67 Illustration by Sarah Kensington. 68 Zev Radovan. 69 Zev Radovan, T, BR. 70 Zev Radovan. 71 Illustration by Sarah Kensington. 72 BLMJ Borowski Collection/Zev Radovan. 73 Zev Radovan, TL, MR; Illustration by Gill Tomblin. 74 Zev Radovan, TR, BL. 75 Illustration by Peter Morter. 76 Illustration by Ed Dorey. 77 British Museum, London/Michael Holford. 78 Archaeological Museum, Istanbul/AKG/Eric Lessing. 79 Werner Forman Achive. 80-81 Illustration by Terence Dalley. 81 Zev Radovan. 82 British Museum, London. 83 Illustration by Gill Tomblin. 84 *Ploughing*, from *Book of the Dead*, British Museum, London, T; Musée du Louvre, Paris, BL. 85 AAAC/Ronald Sheridan, TL; Artwork by TBA, TR; Zev Radovan, BL. 86 British Museum, London/BAL. 87 British Museum, London. 88 TBA. 89 Bildarchiv Foto Marburg, T; BLMJ Borowski Collection/Zev Radovan, BL. 90-91 Illustration by Sarah Kensington. 92 Illustration by Sarah Kensington. 93 Sonia Halliday Photographs, TR; Musée du Louvre, Paris, BL. 94 TBA, BL. 94-95 Illustration by Sarah Kensington. 95 British Museum, London. 96 National Archaeological Museum, Beirut/Eric Lessing. 97 Illustration by Sarah Kensington. 98 British Museum, London/Michael Holford. 99 University Museum, University of Pennsylvania. 100 Musée du Louvre, Paris/E.T. Archive, TL; Musée du Louvre, Paris/Michael Holford, TR. 101 Musée du Louvre, Paris/BAL, BL; Illustration by Christian Hook, TR. 102 Musée du Louvre, Paris/AKG/Eric Lessing. 103 British Museum, London/Michael Holford. 104-5 Illustration by Peter Morter. 106 British Museum, London. 107 AAAC/Ronald Sheridan, T; Musée du Louvre/Bulloz, BR. 108 British Museum, London/AKG/Eric Lessing. 109 British Museum, London/Michael Holford, T; Illustration by Sarah Kensington, B. 110-11 Illustration by Peter Morter. 111 AAAC/Ronald Sheridan, T. 112 Illustration by Gill Tomblin. 113 British Museum, London/AKG/Eric Lessing. 115 Illustration by Sarah Kensington. 116 AAAC/Ronald Sheridan. 117 Zev Radovan, T, B. 118 Zev Radovan. 119 Zev Radovan, T, BR; Illustration by Gill Tomblin, BL. 120 Bildarchiv Foto Marburg. 121 AAAC/Ronald Sheridan. 122 Illustration by Christian Hook. 123, 124, 125 Zev Radovan. 126-7 *Judean Hills*/Sonia Halliday Photographs. 127 British Museum, London, T. 128-9 Illustration by Christian Hook. 130 AAAC/Ronald Sheridan. 131 Zev Radovan, T, B. 132 *Ishtar*, ivory, Metropolitan Museum of Art, New York, T; *The Ark of the Covenant from the Synagogue, Capernaum, Israel*/Sonia Halliday Photographs, ML; AAAC/Ronald Sheridan, BR. 133 British Museum, London. 134 Illustration by Christian Hook. 135 British Museum, London. 136 British Museum, London, TL; Zev Radovan, BR. 137 Egyptian Museum, Cairo/TBA. 138 *River Jordan, Israel*/Sonia Halliday Photographs. 140-1 Illustration by Kevin Goold. 142 Sonia Halliday Photographs. 143 AAAC/Ronald Sheridan. 144 Zev Radovan. 145 *Lion-headed Demon*, yellow alabaster from period of Nebuchadnezzar, Metropolitan Museum of Art, New York, TL; *Pottery Stand from Megiddo*, Oriental Institute, BR. 146 BLMJ Borowski Collection. 147 AAAC/Ronald Sheridan. 148 AAAC/Ronald Sheridan. 149 Illustration by Christian Hook. 150 Werner Forman Archive/Dr. E. Strouhal, TL; Musée du Louvre, Paris/E.T. Archive, TM; Turkish National Museum/Michael Holford, TR; Illustration by Carl Meek, ML; Robert Harding Picture Library, MR; British Museum, London, BL; C.M. Dixon, BM; Knossos, Crete/E.T. Archive, BR. 151 AAAC/Ronald Sheridan, TL; Egyptian Museum, Cairo/E.T. Archive, TM; Egyptian Museum, Cairo/Jürgen Liepe, ML; British Museum, London, MR; Egyptian Museum, Cairo/Giraudon/BAL, BL; Robert Harding Picture Library/John Miller, BR. 152 Werner Forman Archive, TL; C.M. Dixon, TR; Victoria & Albert Museum, London/BAL, ML; AAAC/Ronald Sheridan, MR; Dallas Museum of Art/Werner Forman Archive, BL; AAAC/Ronald Sheridan, BM; Oriental Museum, Durham University/BAL, BR. 153 AAAC/Ronald Sheridan, TL; Musée du Louvre, Paris/Giraudon/BAL, TM; British Museum, London/Michael Holford, TR; British Museum, London/Michael Holford, ML, MR; Robert Harding Picture Library, BL; AAAC/Ronald Sheridan, BM, BR. 154 British Museum, London, TL; C. M. Dixon, TM; AAAC/Ronald Sheridan, TR; Zev Radovan, ML; AAAC, BL; British Museum, London/E.T. Archive, BM; Ephesus Museum, Turkey/E.T. Archive, BR. 155 AAAC/Ronald Sheridan, TL, TM, ML, MM, MR; British Museum, London/E.T. Archive, BL; British Library/E.T. Archive, BR.

Front cover: Illustrations by Gill Tomblin, TL, BM; British Museum/AKG/Eric Lessing, ML; Illustration by Peter Morter, MR; Zev Radovan, BL, BR.

Back cover: British Museum, TL; Zev Radovan, TR, BL; ASAP/Lev Borodulin, M; Illustrations by Gill Tomblin, BM, BR.

The editors are grateful to the following publishers for their kind permission to quote passages from the books below:
Wm. Collins Son & Co. Ltd for the Bible Societies, *The Holy Bible*, Revised Standard Version, 1952, 1971; Division of Christian Education of the National Council of the Churches of Christ in the United States of America, *The Holy Bible,* New Revised Standard Version, 1989; Jewish Publication Society, *Masoretic Text.*